Speaking Amish

A Beginner's Introduction to Pennsylvania German

for ages 10 to 100

Lillian Stoltzfus

Photography by Daniel Stoltzfus and Lillian Stoltzfus

Speaking Amish

A Beginner's Introduction to Pennsylvania German

 Published by

Eckschank

Publishing

ISBN 978-1-60126-372-8

Library of Congress Control Number: 2012956521

Table of Contents

Pennsylvania German

Pennsylvania German is spoken throughout the United States and Canada. Although people from each region can understand each other, each region speaks it a little differently. The Pennsylvania German in this book is specifically how it is spoken by the Amish in Lancaster County. Maybe even more specifically, by the Amish in my family! I took the liberty of using a few words that most people do not use anymore - words that my grandmother might have used. This book is designed to be "descriptive" of Pennsylvania German, not "prescriptive." I have tried to portray how it *is* spoken, not how it *should* be spoken.

*Most of the names in this book are fictitious.

Acknowledgements

For the majority of the words, I used the spelling from C. Richard Beam and Jennifer L. Trout's *The Comprehensive Pennsylvania German Dictionary*. The spelling for "far" (Lesson 6), "Schtories" (Lesson 9), "Dallbopp" and "Dallbobbe" (Lesson 10), "Bobbli" and "Bobblin" (Lesson 13), "neegscht" (Lesson 21), and "Bank" and "Benk" (Lesson 22) come from Eugene S. Stine's *Pennsylvania German Dictionary*. I relied mostly on *The Comprehensive Pennsylvania German Dictionary* for the spelling of the verbs and their conjugations.

I added "Gut Mann" (Lesson 12) and "Warte" (Lesson 9) and changed the spelling of "Midde" to "Midd" (Lesson 22), to reflect how my family uses those words. The word "pivvich" (Lesson 15) was in neither of those dictionaries so I created my own spelling and definition. In a few cases, I used my own definitions which I felt more accurately described how the words are used in Lancaster County. These words are marked with a $^{+}$ symbol.

For the grammar and phonics tips, I used J. William Frey's *A Simple Grammar of Pennsylvania Dutch* and also Joshua R. Brown and Douglas J. Madenford's *Schwetz Mol Deitsch* as resources.

Thank You

God: You are the origin of all creativity, and I am grateful to you for giving me the ability to produce this book.

Dad: Your photography needs a bigger stage, and I am thrilled that my book can be that stage. Thank you for giving me free access to your trove of great photographs. Thanks also for trusting me with your expensive photography equipment and allowing me to gallivant around Lancaster County with it.

Mom: Thank you for your excitement and valuable suggestions for my book. Your encouragement kept me going when I was ready to quit.

Katie Stoltzfus: Thank you for using your expertise to find my Pennsylvania German grammar errors and to polish the culture tips.

Melanie Beiler: Thank you for reviewing my book from a non-Pennsylvania German speaker's perspective.

Susan Lapp: Thank you for taking time away from your wedding preparation to do the final edit for this book. Because of you, I feel more confident about sending this book to the printer.

Suggestions for Learning Pennsylvania German

Enjoy the loan words.

The words in dark blue are "loan words." They are borrowed from the English language and follow English spelling rules instead of Pennsylvania German spelling rules. Because all nouns in German are capitalized, the English nouns are also capitalized.

Make lots of flashcards.

Get a stack of 5" x 7" cards. Write the English word on one side and the German word on the other side. Writing an English pronunciation equivalent of the word on the flashcards might be helpful. For example, for the word "Daett," write "Datt" beside it since that is more as it sounds in English.

Practice the flashcards.

At first, put only about ten new words in the flashcard stack. Practice them until you know them. Then add five new words to the stack. Try to remember the old words *and* learn the new words.

If you know a word **very** well, take it out of the flashcard stack and put it in a box marked "Learned Words." Every several weeks, take the flashcards out and see if you still remember them. If you forgot any of them, put them back in the flashcard stack again until you learn it.

If possible, practice your flashcards with a *native speaker*. A native speaker is someone who learned the language when they were young. Native speakers have the correct accent and will tell you if the word is pronounced correctly.

Do not think every word has to be learned perfectly before going to the next lesson, but try to memorize *most* of the words. Every lesson uses words from the lessons before it.

Learn the verbs by using the verb charts.

The verbs are probably the most difficult thing about German. To make it easier, do not make flashcards with the verbs. Instead, use the big verb charts at the back of the book. Copy them and hang them on your wall or on your sink or on the dash of your car.

Say the pronouns and verbs together, just as on the CD: "Ich bin," "Du bischt," etc. Say them over and over again. Next, see if you can make sentences with the phrases. Examples: "Ich bin dinn." "Du bischt gut." "Er iss gross."

At first, follow along in the book while listening to the CD.

This will help you read German. Do not think you have to understand everything right away. If a Grammar Tip seems difficult, skip over it and go to the next lesson. Come back to the difficult lesson another day, and it may make more sense.

If you are ambitious, and want to be able to **read** Pennsylvania German right away, peek ahead to the next lessons and study the Phonics Tips to help you become a better reader. Or use the Phonics Chart at the back of the book.

Later, listen to the CD while you do other things.

Listen to the CD over and over. Listen to it while you are doing chores or while you are on the road. Maybe you can download it onto your MP3 player.

Practice all the words you know.

Speak as much Pennsylvania German as possible. If your grandma or aunt are native speakers, say words to them in Pennsylvania German. Talk to the dog in Pennsylvania German.

Do not worry if people laugh at you.

If your Amish relatives or neighbors laugh at you when you are trying to speak Pennsylvania German, just laugh with them. If they are laughing at you, that means you are trying, and people who try learn very quickly. After awhile they will see how much you are learning, and they will stop laughing.

Remember: **"The more they are laughing, the more you are learning!"**

Subject Pronouns							
ich	**du**	**er**	**sie**	**es**	**mir**	**dihr**	**sie**
I	you [s]	he	she	it	we	you [p]	they

[s]= singular (one) **[p]= plural** (more than one)

(der) Bauwer farmer		fett fat	
(die) Hausfraa [p] Hausweiwer housewife		dinn thin	
(es) Yaahr [p] Yaahre year		alt old	
(der) Daett Dad		siwwe seven	
(die) Maem Mom		acht eight	

Lesson 1
Introductions

John: Ich bin der John. (I am John.)

Susie: Ich bin die Susie. (I am Susie.)

John: Ich bin siwwe Yaahr alt. (I am seven years old.)

Susie: Ich bin acht Yaahr alt. (I am eight years old.)

John/Susie: Mir sin Amish. (We are Amish.)

John: Susie, du bischt fett. (Susie, you are fat.)

Susie: Ich bin net fett! (I am not fat!) Ich bin dinn! (I am thin!)

John: Mei Daett iss en Bauwer. (My dad is a farmer.) Er iss net alt. (He is not old.)

Susie: Mei Maem iss en Hausfraa. (My mom is a housewife.)

Sie iss net alt. (She is not old.)

John: Sie sin Amish. (They are Amish.)

Aunt Lill (to all who are studying this lesson):

Dihr sint net alt.

(You are not old.)

Other Words	
mei	my
en	a, an
die, der, es	the
net	not

Verb		
sei (to be)		
ich	bin	I am
du	bi**scht**	you [s] are
er, sie, es	iss	he/she/it is
mir	sin	we are
dihr	sin**t**	you [p] are
sie	sin	they are

Phonics Tips

In Lancaster County, when the letter "r" comes at the beginning of a word or between two vowels (a, e, i, o, or u), it is pronounced just like the English letter "r," and in Ohio or western Pennsylvania, it is pronounced like the Spanish rolled "r."[1]

Most of the time, the "w" in Pennsylvania German has the "v" sound.[2]

Examples:

Hausweiwer (housewives) - say "Hausveiver"   siwwe (seven) - say "sivve"

There are some exceptions to this rule. Listen carefully to the CD to learn the new words.

Grammar Tip

In Pennsylvania German, nouns are either **feminine, masculine**, or **neuter.**[3] Every time Pennsylvania German speakers want to use the word "**the**" before a noun, they have to make sure they use the correct word for "**the**" with it, depending on whether it is feminine, masculine, or neuter. There are three words for the: **die**, **der**, or **es**. This is easy when one is speaking about people.

Use "**die**" if the noun is **feminine** (a girl or woman).

Use "**der**" if the noun is **masculine** (a boy or man).

Use "**es**" if it is **neuter** (neither masculine or feminine).

When talking about someone, always add "die" or "der" in front of their name.

Example:

Die Mary iss alt. (Mary is old.)   Der John iss net alt. (John is not old.)

In the Vocabulary Charts, the nouns have the correct word (die, der, or es) in front of them. When memorizing the noun, memorize the correct word for "the" along with it.

Er iss en Bauwer.

Exercises

A. Fill in the blank with the correct form of "the" (die, der, es).

1. _____ John iss net alt.
2. _____ Mary iss dinn.
3. _____ Maem iss en Hausfraa.
4. _____ Daett iss en Bauwer.

B. Introduce yourself. Use "die" if you are female and "der" if you are male.

Examples: Ich bin die Susie. Ich bin der John.

____.

C. Use the verb chart to fill in the correct form of the verb "bin."

1. Ich ______ dinn.
2. Mir ______ Amish.
3. Sie (she) ______ net fett.
4. Dihr ______ alt.
5. Er ______ net Amish.
6. Du ______ dinn.
7. Sie (they) ______alt.

Culture Tip

Most Amish women are housewives. They stay at home and take care of the children and the house. During the summer, they work in their gardens and preserve a lot of food. In the winter, they sew clothes for their family. Occasionally, they work away from home in a family business such as a market stand.

Years ago, most Amish men were farmers. Because the land is more scarce today, many men work away from home on carpenter crews, in sawmills, etc. Others have home businesses and sell things such as storage barns, furniture, or crafts.

Learning Pennsylvania German Verbs

Verbs in Pennsylvania German can be tricky. But they are easier than they look. In the first lesson, we had an irregular verb, which means the verb did not follow a pattern. Unfortunately, irregular verbs will need to be memorized.

The great thing is that many of the verbs are regular. That means they follow a pattern. The verb in the next lesson is regular. Let's take a look at it.

Verb		
gleiche (to like)		
ich	gleich	I like
du	gleich**scht**	you [s] like
er, sie, es	gleich**t**	he, she, it likes
mir	gleich**e**	we like
dihr	gleich**et**	you [p] like
sie	gleich**e**	they like

(ich, du, er/sie/es: one person)

(mir, dihr, sie: more than one person)

Notice that the beginning of this word is "gleich" for every single person or people. Just add the correct ending, depending whom one talks to or about.

Sie gleiche der Camel.

Most regular verbs have one syllable as the root word. This one has the root "gleich." To remember which ending to use: when talking to **one** person, add extra sounds to the verb, but not extra syllables. For example, to talk *to* **one person,** add the "scht" sound; and to talk *about* **one person**, add the "t" sound. The amount of syllables does not change.

However, when talking to or about **more** than one person, add an extra *syllable* to the verb. For example, to talk directly *to* **more than one person**, add an extra "et" which creates an extra syllable. When talking *about* **more than one person**, add an extra "e" which creates an extra syllable. When talking about **yourself and another person**, add an extra "e" which creates an extra syllable.

Remember: **One person = one syllable** **more than one person = more than one syllable**

(In this book, only one regular verb does not follow the above rule, and that is the verb in Lesson 7: schtudie. For that verb, one person has two syllables, and more than one person has three syllables.)

Only eight of the verbs in this book are irregular. Those are the ones that should be studied most. When using the verb charts, put all the regular verbs together in one group and all the irregular verbs in the other group. Concentrate mostly on the irregular verbs, because the regular verbs will become automatic. The irregular verbs are from Lessons 1, 3, 4, 8, 11, 14, 16, and 20: **be, have, go, do, write, stand, want,** and **give.**

* Just for the record: Amish do not normally raise camels, but one family in Lancaster County does!

(es) Bissel

bit

(der) Kuche

cake

(es) Ess-sach

food

yung

young

(der) Appel

[p] Eppel

apple

gut

good

well

(es) Deitsch

German

glee

little

(der) Boi

pie

schmaert

smart

Other Words	
un	and
awwer	but, so

Lesson 2 - Things We Like

John: Susie, du bischt alt. (Susie, you are old.)

Susie: Ich bin net alt! (I am not old.) Ich bin yung. (I am young.)

John/Susie: Mir gleiche gut Ess-sach. (We like good food.)

John: Ich gleich Cookies. (I like cookies.)

Susie: Ich gleich en Bissel Kuche. (*I like a bit cake*. I like a bit of cake.)

John: Susie, du gleischt Pudding. (Susie, you like pudding.)

Susie: Der Daett gleicht Eppel Boi, awwer er iss net fett. (Dad likes apple pie, but he is not fat.)

John: Die Maem gleicht Shoo-fly Boi, un sie iss en glee Bissel fett. (Mom likes shoo-fly pie, and she is a little bit fat.)

Susie: Die Maem un der Daett gleiche Chocolate Candy. (Mom and Dad like chocolate candy.)

Aunt Lill (to all who are studying this lesson):

Dihr gleichet Pennsylvania Deitsch. (You like Pennsylvania German.)

Dihr sint schmaert! (You are smart!)

Verb		
gleiche (to like)		
ich	gleich	I like
du	gleich**scht**	you like
er, sie, es	gleich**t**	he/she/it likes
mir	gleich**e**	we like
dihr	gleich**et**	you like
sie	gleich**e**	they like

Sie gleicht Soda.

Er iss alt.

Phonics Tip

When "r" comes in the middle or at the end of a word, it usually has the "ah" sound.[4] See an exception in Lesson 4.

Examples:

mir (we) - say "mee-ah"   dihr (you [p]) - say "dee-ah"

Sometimes the "r" is silent.

Example:

der (the) - say "de"

Grammar Tip

Remembering that a noun is either **masculine**, **feminine**, or **neuter** is easy when one is talking about people. But Pennsylvania German can be tricky. "Cake" and "apple" both have "der" in front of them, but "food" has "es" in front of it. To say that a cake and an apple are **masculine** and that food is **neuter** seems strange. Oh well, grammar is strange sometimes.

When a noun is plural (more than one), things get easier. **Always** use "**die**" when the noun is plural, even if the word is usually **masculine** or **neuter**.

Examples:

Ich gleich **die** Kuche. (I like the cakes.)

Er gleicht **die** Eppel. (He likes the apples.)

Der John un die Susie gleiche **die** Boi. (*The John and the Susie like the pies*. John and Susie like the pies.)

Remember:

use "**der**" for **masculine** (a boy or man)

use "**die**" for **feminine** (a girl or woman)

use "**es**" for **neuter** (neither masculine or feminine)

use "**die**" for **plural** (more than one of *anything*)

Do not worry too much about remembering the "**der**" and "**die**" and "**es**" perfectly. Native speakers do not always say them correctly either. Listen to the CD over and over again, and soon the correct word for "the" will come naturally.

Culture Tip

Amish women know how to make pies with flaky crusts, smooth puddings, moist cakes, whoopie pies, and other desserts. Maybe that is why Susie and John's mom is a little bit fat. Calling someone "fat" is not polite, though! Maybe Mom was out in the field helping Dad when John and Susie had this conversation.

Exercises

A. Use the verb chart to fill in the correct form of the verb "gleich."

1. Ich ____________ Kuche.
2. Mir ____________ Eppel.
3. Sie (she) ___________ der Daett.
4. Dihr ____________ Cookies.
5. Er ____________ Boi.
6. Du ___________Pudding.
7. Sie (they) __________Ess-sach.

B. Translate the sentences in A.

Sie sin yung.

(der) Schpringwaage spring wagon		(der) Nochber [p] Nochbere neighbor	
(der) Gaul [p] Geil horse		bloh blue	
(es) Dachweggeli [p] Dachweggelin buggy		rot red	
(die) Maschien [p] Maschiene engine car+		gross big	

Verb	
hawwe (to have)	
ich	hab (hawwich)
du	ho**scht**
er, sie, es	ho**t**
mir	hen
dihr	hen**t**
sie	hen

Other Words	
aa	also
ya	yes

See Lesson 7 for an explanation of the words in parentheses in the verb chart after the "ich."

Lesson 3 - Things We Own

John: Ich hab en Scooter. (I have a scooter.) Mei Scooter iss rot. (My scooter is red.) *Es iss gross. (It is big.)

Susie, du hoscht aa en Scooter. (*Susie, you have also a scooter*. Susie, you also have a scooter.)

Susie: Ya, ich hab aa en Scooter. (*Yes, I have also a scooter*. Yes, I also have a scooter.)

Mei Scooter iss net bloh. (My scooter is not blue.) *Es iss rot. (It is red.)

*Es iss glee. (It is little.) Ich gleich mei Scooter. (I like my scooter.)

John: Der Daett hot en Schpringwaage. (Dad has a spring wagon.)

En Bauwer gleicht en Schpringwaage. (A farmer likes a spring wagon.)

Susie: Mir hen net en Maschien. (*We have not a car*. We do not have a car.)

Mir hen en Gaul un en Dachweggeli. (We have a horse and a buggy.)

John: Mir gleiche en Dachweggeli. (We like a buggy.)

Susie: Die Nochbere sin Amish. (The neighbors are Amish.)

Sie hen aa net en Maschien. (*They have also not a car*. They also do not have a car.)

John: Sie gleiche net en Maschien. (*They like not a car*. They do not like a car.)

Sie gleiche en Gaul un en Dachweggeli.

(They like a horse and a buggy.)

Aunt Lill (to all who are studying this lesson):

Dihr hent en Maschien. (You have a car.)

Dihr gleichet en Maschien. (You like a car.)

> "Dach" is a roof and "Weggeli" is a little wagon. "Dachweggeli" literally means "little roof wagon." Doesn't a buggy look like a wagon with a roof?

Er hot en Scooter.

*Some speakers might use the word "er" instead of "es" in these sentences, because they consider "Scooter" to be a masculine noun, and they are making the pronoun agree with the noun.

Er hot en Wagge.

Phonics Tip

Amish people in Lancaster County like to do things fast. When they use the word "**es**," they do not pronounce the "e" sound. A sentence such as "Es iss gross" (It is big) sounds like "**s iss** gross."

If this seems difficult, imagine what Germans think when they study English!

See Lesson 8 for an explanation of pronouncing "Waage."

Grammar Tip

To negate a sentence (make a sentence say not) is very easy in German. Just add the word "net" (not) after the verb.

Examples:

"Mir **hen** en Maschien." (We have a car.)

"Mir **hen** *net* en Maschien." (*We have not a car.* We do not have a car.)

"Ich **gleich** Cookies." (I like cookies.)

"Ich **gleich** *net* Cookies." (*I like not cookies.* I do not like cookies.)

"Ich **bin** dinn." (I am thin.)

"Ich **bin** *net* dinn." (I am not thin.)

Culture Tip

The Amish usually go to church with their horse and buggy. A farmer will likely also own a spring wagon. He uses this like a pickup truck to haul things when he doesn't want to get his buggy dirty.

Exercises

A. Use the verb chart to fill in the correct form of the verb "hawwe."

1. Ich _____ net en Gaul.
2. Sie (they) ______ siwwe Eppel.
3. Sie (she) ________ en Gaul.
4. Dihr ________ gut Ess-sach.
5. Mir ________ en Kuche.
6. Du _______en Schpringwaage.
7. Er ________ net en Maschien.

B. Make the following sentences negative.

1. Ich hab drei Kuche.

____

2. Sie hen en Maschien.

____

3. Dihr hent acht Nochbere.

____

C. Translate the new sentences in B.

Er hot en Gaul.

(die) Vendyu [p] Vendyu auction		schtarck fast, swiftly strong	
(die) Gmee [p] Gmeene church		langsam slow slowly	
(die) Schul [p] Schule school		wunderbaar wonderful	

Verb	
geh (to go)	
ich	geh (gehn ich)
du	geh**scht**
er, sie, es	geh**t**
mir	geh**n**
dihr	geh**nt**
sie	geh**n**

Other Words	
zu	to
mit	with
ebmols	sometimes
fatt	away from home

Lesson 4
Going Away

John: Ich geh zu die Schul mit mei Scooter. (I go to school with my scooter.)

Susie: Ich geh aa zu die Schul mit mei Scooter. (*I go also to the school with my scooter.* I also go to school with my scooter.)

John: Mir gehn langsam. (We go slowly.)

Susie: Der Daett geht zu die Vendyu mit der Schpringwaage. (He goes to the auction with the spring wagon.)

John: Mir gehn zu die Gmee mit der Gaul un es Dachweggeli. (We go to church with the horse and buggy.)

Der Gaul geht schtarck. (The horse goes fast.)

Er iss wunderbaar. (He is wonderful.)

Susie: Die Nochbere hen aa en Gaul un en Dachweggeli. (*The neighbors have also a horse and a buggy*. The neighbors also have a horse and buggy.)

Sie gehn zu die Gmee mit der Gaul un es Dachweggeli. (They go to church with the horse and buggy.)

John: Mir gehn ebmols fatt mit en Driver. *(We go sometimes away with a driver.* We go away sometimes with a driver.)

Susie: Der Driver iss English.* (The driver is English.)

John: Er hot en Maschien. (He has a car.)

Susie: Ich gleich en Maschien net! (*I like a car not!* I do not like a car!)

Ich gleich en Gaul un en Dachweggeli. (I like a horse and buggy.)

Aunt Lill (to all who are studying this lesson):

Dihr gehnt schtarck mit en Maschien. (You go fast with a car.)

Mir gehn langsam mit en Dachweggeli. (We go slowly with a buggy.)

*To an Amish person, anyone who is not Amish is "English."

Phonics Tip

The "r" is silent when it follows the short "a" sound and precedes a consonant.[5] There are some exceptions, like the word "schtarck" in this lesson, where the "r" is pronounced like the English "r."

Example:

Wart (word) - say "Vat"

Grammar Tip

In the last lesson, we learned that to negate a sentence, we add the word "net" right after the verb.

To *really* emphasize that you do not like something, use the word "net" at the **end** of the sentence.

Examples:

"Ich **gleich** die Schul *net*!" (*I like the school not!* I do not like school.)

"Ich **gleich** Cookies *net*!" (*I like cookies not!* I do not like cookies!)

See Lesson 7 for an explanation for the words in parentheses in the verb chart after "ich."

Sie geht fatt mit die Maem un der Daett.

Culture Tip

The Amish do not own cars, but they are allowed to go away with a car if an "English" person is driving. When I was a little girl, I did not like to go away with a car because I got carsick. A horse and buggy was much better.

Exercises

A. Use the verb chart to fill in the correct form of the verb "geh."

1. Ich ________ mit der Daett.
2. Dihr ________ zu die Vendyu.
3. Sie (she) ________ mit die Maem.
4. Sie (they) ________ net mit en Maschien.
5. Mir ________ fatt.
6. Du ________ zu die Gmee.
7. Er ________ mit der Gaul.

B. The following sentences are negative. Give them extra emphasis by putting the "net" at the end of the sentence.

1. Sie gleiche net en Schpringwaage.

____

2. Er gleicht net Eppel.

____

3. Ich gleich net Shoo-fly Boi.

____

C. Translate the sentences in B.

Sie gehn fatt mit Scooters.

(die) Scheier

[p] Scheiere

barn

(der) Dreck

dirt

(die) Kich

[p] Kiche

kitchen

weech

soft

(der) Gaarde

garden

hatt

hard

(die) Kuh

[p] Kieh

cow

Other Words	
sell, seller, selli *	that
zammer	together
allfatt	always

Verb	
schaffe (to work)	
ich	schaff
du	schaff**scht**
er, sie, es	schaff**t**
mir	schaff**e**
dihr	schaff**et**
sie	schaff**e**

*See Lesson 24 for a more complete explanation of "sell", "seller" and "selli."

Lesson 5 - Working

John: Ich schaff hatt in die Scheier. (I work hard in the barn.)

Ich schaff mit die Kieh un die Geil. (I work with the cows and the horses.)

Susie: Mir hen siwwe Geil. (We have seven horses.)

John: Ich gleich die Geil. (I like the horses.)

Susie, du schaffscht in die Kich. (Susie, you work in the kitchen.)

Susie: Ya, ich schaff in die Kich. (Yes, I work in the kitchen.)

Die Maem schafft aa in die Kich. (*The mom works also in the kitchen*. Mom also works in the kitchen.)

Ebmols schaffe mir zammer. (*Sometimes work we together.* Sometimes we work together.)

Ich gleich sell. (I like that.)

John: Der Daett un die Maem schaffe in der Gaarde. (Dad and Mom work in the garden.)

Der Gaarde iss gross. (The garden is big.)

Susie: Die Maem un der Daett schaffe in der weech Dreck. (Mom and Dad work in the soft dirt.)

Sie schaffe zammer. (They work together.)

John: Sie schaffe net langsam. (*They work not slowly*. They do not work slowly.)

Sie schaffe schtarck. (They work fast.)

Aunt Lill (to all who are studying this lesson):

Dihr schaffet allfatt hatt mit Deitsch.

(*You work always hard with German*.

You always work hard with German.)

Sell iss gut. (That is good.)

Dihr schaffet zammer.

(You work together.)

Phonics Tip

The "sch" in Pennsylvania German has the "sh" sound.[6] Why does it have an extra letter? I think the "c" wants to be noticed even when it does not make a sound. What a proud little letter!

Examples:

schaffe (to work) - say "shaffe"

Scheier (barn) - say "sheier"

Grammar Tip

When using an adverb (a word that says how, when or where) or adverb phrase **at the beginning of a sentence**, something very strange happens in Pennsylvania German: the verb (action or being word) comes first instead of the noun or pronoun![7]

ebmols

Verb	
schaffe (to work)	
ich	schaff
du	schaff**scht**
er, sie	schaff**t**
mir	schaff**e**
dihr	schaff**et**
sie	schaff**e**

Example:

"*Ebmols* **schaff** ich hatt." (*Sometimes work I hard.* Sometimes I work hard.)

"*Ebmols* **schaffscht** du in der Gaarde." (*Sometimes work you in the garden.* Sometimes you work in the garden.)

Der Daett un die Maem schaffe zammer in der Gaarde.

Sie schaffe hatt.

Exercises

A. Use the verb chart to fill in the correct form of the verb "schaffe."

1. Ich ____________ schtarck.
2. Sie (they) ____________ in die Scheier.
3. Mir ____________ in die Schul.
4. Sie (she) ____________ mit die Nochbere.
5. Dihr ____________ in die Kich.
6. Du ____________ mit die Geil.
7. Er ____________ langsam.

B. Change the following sentences by putting the word in bold print first. Make sure you change the noun and the pronoun correctly.

1. Ich bin langsam **ebmols**.

____

2. Sie schaffe hatt **allfatt**.

____

Culture Tip

Amish ladies have a lot of peer pressure to keep a beautiful garden. When my Amish aunts come to visit our house, they take a tour of the garden and the flower beds, and "ooh" and "aah" over anything that strikes their fancy. If they see a particularly beautiful flower, they might ask for a starter root, and next year we will see it in their garden.

(die) Buhn [p] Buhne bean		(die) Grummbier [p] Grummbiere potatoes	
(es) Dunkes gravy		gschtampt mashed	
(es) Fleesch meat		hungerich hungry	
(der) Eppelsaes applesauce		kusslich prone to soil with food	
(es) Welschkann corn			

Other Words	
far	for
nau	now

Verb	
esse (to eat)	
ich	ess
du	es**scht**
er, sie, es	ess**t**
mir	ess**e**
dihr	ess**et**
sie	ess**e**

Lesson 6 - Eating

John: Mir schaffe hatt. (We work hard.)

Susie: Nau sin mir hungerich. (*Now are we hungry*. Now we are hungry.)

Mir esse gschtampti Grummbiere far Supper. (We eat mashed potatoes for supper.)

John: Mir hen aa Fleesch un Buhne un Welschkann. (*We have also meat and beans and corn*. We also have chicken and beans and corn.)

Ich ess allfatt Dunkes mit gschtampti Grummbiere. (*I eat always gravy with mashed potatoes*. I always eat gravy with mashed potatoes.)

Susie, esscht du Dunkes mit gschtampti Grummbiere? (*Susie, eat you gravy with mashed potatoes*? Susie, do you eat gravy with mashed potatoes?)

Susie: Ya, es iss gut. (Yes, it is good.)

John: Der Daett esst Eppelsaes mit gschtampti Grummbiere. (Dad eats apple sauce with mashed potatoes.)

Susie: Ich gleich sell net! (*I like that not!* I don't like that!)

Der Daett un der John esse en lot. (Dad and John eat a lot.)

John, du bischt kusslich! (John, you are messy!) Du esscht schtarck. (You eat fast.)

John: Ich bin net kusslich! (I am not messy!) Ich ess net schtarck! (*I eat not fast!* I do not eat fast!)

Aunt Lill (to all who are studying this lesson):

Nau sin dihr aa hungerich. (*Now are you also hungry*. Now you are also hungry.)

Esset dihr en lot? (*Eat you a lot?* Do you eat a lot?)

*See Lesson 10 for an explanation of why there is an "i" at the end of "gschtampt."

> "Kusslich" cannot be neatly translated with one word into English. It means being messy when you eat. When toddlers are learning to eat, they are "kusslich."

Sie esst Welschkann.

Phonics Tip

The "ch" can have two different sounds, depending which letter it follows. When "ch" comes after "ei," "ie," or "i," it has the "h" sound, as in the English word "human."[8]

Examples:

gleich (like) - say "gleih"   hungerich (hungry) - say "hungerih"

When "ch" comes after "a," "o," "u," or "ou," it has a strange guttural sound, almost like something is stuck in your throat.[9]

Examples:

acht (eight)   Kuche (cake)

Listen to the CD and to native speakers and try to imitate them!

Grammar Tip

To ask a question in Pennsylvania German, look at the verb chart and switch the pronouns and the verbs, just like the previous lesson with the adverbs or adverb phrases. Say the **verb** first, not the pronoun.[10]

Examples:

"**Esscht** du Grummbiere?" (*Eat you potatoes?* Do you eat potatoes?)

"**Esst** sie Kuche?" (*Eats she cake*? Does she eat cake?)

"**Esset** dihr en lot?" (*Eat you a lot?* Do you eat a lot?)

Verb	
esse (to eat)	
ich	ess
du	es**scht**
er, sie, es	ess**t**
mir	ess**e**
dihr	ess**et**
sie	ess**e**

When asking a question with "net" (not) in it, make sure to say the "net" *after* the verb and noun or pronoun.

Examples:

"**Schaffscht** du *net* hatt?" (*Work you not hard*?

Don't you work hard?)

"**Hot** der Henry *net* en Gaul?" (*Has the Henry not a horse?* Doesn't Henry have a horse?)

Sie esse en lot Boi.

Sie esse in die Kich.

Exercises

A. Use the verb chart to fill in the correct form of the verb "esse."

1. Ich ___________ Grummbiere.
2. Sie (they) ___________ Kuche.
3. Sie (she) ___________ Fleesch.
4. Dihr ___________ der Eppelsaes.
5. Mir ___________ es Ess-sach.
6. Du ___________ die Eppel.
7. Er ___________ schtarck.

B. Change the following sentences into questions. Make sure you place the noun and verb in the correct order.

1. Du esscht gschtampti Grummbiere.

____

2. Er esst en lot Kuche.

____

Culture Tip

Amish people eat breakfast in the morning, dinner at noon, and supper in the evening. Everybody sits around the table. They do not pray out loud before the meal. Instead, everybody puts their hands under the table and prays silently until Dad clears his throat or pushes his chair back, which is the signal that the prayer is over.

(es) Kind

[p] Kinner

children

weltlich

worldly

(es) Buch

[p] Bicher

book

katz

short

(es) Licht

[p] Lichter

light

lang

tall[+]

(die) Sunn

[p] Sunne

sun

freindlich

friendly

(die) Schpass

fun

Other Words	
genunk	enough
zu	too
ken	no

Verb	
schtudie (to study)	
ich	schtudi
du	schtudi**scht**
er, sie, es	schtudi**t**
mir	schtudi**e**
dihr	schtudi**et**
sie	schtudi**e**

Lesson 7 – Going to School

John: Die Susie un ich gehn zu die Schul. (Susie and I go to school.)

Susie: Mir schtudie die Bicher. (We study the books.)

John: Mir schtudie hatt. (We study hard.)

Susie: Die Mary Ann iss mei Buddy in die Schul. (Mary Ann is my buddy in school.) Sie iss katz. (She is short.)

Sie iss en lot Schpass.* (*She is a lot fun.* She is a lot of fun.)

Ebmols schtudi ich mit die Mary Ann. (*Sometimes study I with the Mary Ann*. Sometimes I study with Mary Ann.)

John: Mei Buddy Davy iss freindlich. (My buddy Davy is friendly.)

Er iss lang. (He is tall.)

Susie: Der Davy iss schmaert, awwer er schtudit net hatt genunk. (*The Davy is smart, but he studies not hard enough*. Davy is smart, but he does not study hard enough.)

John, du schtudischt hatt. (John, you study hard.)

John: Ya, ich schtudi hatt. (Yes, I study hard.)

Susie: Die Kinner in die Schul schtudie Reading, Writing, un Arithmetic. (The children in the school study reading, writing, and arithmetic.)

John: Sie schtudie net Science. (*They study not science*. They don't study science.)

Sell iss zu weltlich. (That is too worldly.)

Susie: Die Schul hot ken electric Licht. (The school has no electric light.)

Die Sunn iss es Licht. (The sun is the light.)

Aunt Lill (to all who are studying this lesson):

Dihr schtudiet net Deitch in die Schul. (*You study not German in the school.* You don't study German in school.)

Dihr schtudiet English. (You study English.)

*"Sie iss en lot Schpass," is something your modern Amish relatives might not say. My Grandmother used the word "Schpass", but today people often use the word "fun" instead. If you have an Amish Grandmother, she might be impressed if you use the word "Schpass!"

Sie schtudie in die Schul.

Phonics Tip

At the beginning of a word, the "b," "d," and "g" are just like English. In the end of a word, they sound like "p," "t," or "k."[11]

Examples:

Daag (day) - say "daak"

hab (have) - say "hop"

Kind (child) - say "kint"

Advanced Grammar Tip

In a few cases, when the noun and verb are reversed (as in the last two lessons), the verb changes a little.[12] If this is the case, it is shown on the verb charts by the phrase in parentheses (see verb charts in Lessons 3, 4, 8, and 14). This happens occasionally with the pronoun "I," and in only a few verbs.

Examples:

"Nau **gehn** ich zu die Scheier." (*Now go I to the barn.* Now I go to the barn.)

"Ebmols **hawwich** Hinkel far Supper." (*Sometimes have I chicken for supper.* Sometimes I have chicken for supper.)

Culture Tip

Most Amish children go to a school without electricity. The school house has lots of windows to let in the sunshine. On cloudy days, the teacher will light a gas light.

The children study math, English, reading, spelling, geography, vocabulary, health, history, and High German. They do not study Science.

When they are in ninth grade, they only go to school for a half day each week. High German is especially emphasized. Amish children never formally study Pennsylvania German.

Exercises

A. Use the verb chart to fill in the correct form of the verb "schtudie."

1. Sie (she) ___________ in die Schul.
2. Er ___________ es Buch.
3. Ich ________ mit die Kinner.
4. Du ___________ net in Deitsch.
5. Mir ___________ zammer.
6. Dihr ___________ hatt ebmols.
7. Sie (they) ___________ die Bicher.

B. Translate the sentences in A.

Most Amish schools do not use indoor plumbing. Instead, they use outdoor toilets like this one for their restroom.

(der) Daag [p] Daage day		recht right	4 + 4 = 8
(die) Arwet work		schlappich sloppy	
dumm dumb		schee beautiful pretty nice	

Other Words	
yo	yes
alle	every+
heit	today
alles	everything
all	all

Verb	
duh (to do)	
ich	duh (duhn ich)
du	du**scht**
er, sie, es	du**tt**
mir	die**n**
dihr	dien**t**
sie	die**n**

Lesson 8 – Doing Good Work at School

John: Ich duh mei Lessons recht in die Schul. (I do my lessons correctly in school.)

Susie: Mei Buddy Mary Ann dutt alles recht. (My buddy Mary Ann does everything right.)

Sie iss net dumm. (She is not stupid.) Sie iss schmaert. (She is smart.)

John: All die Kinner dien gut Arwet heit. (All the children do good work today.)

Susie: Ebmols dien sie net gut Arwet. (*Sometimes do they not good work*. Sometimes they do not do good work.)

Sie schaffe langsam. (They work slowly.)

John: Susie, du duscht ebmols schlappich Arwet. (*Susie, you do sometimes sloppy work.* Susie, sometimes you do sloppy work.)

Susie: Ich duh net! (I do not!) Ich duh schee Arwet. (I do nice work.)

Du duscht net schee Arwet. (*You do not nice work.* You don't do nice work.)

John: Yo, ich duh! (Yes, I do!)

Mei Arwet iss allfatt schee. (My work is always nice.)

Ich duh mei Lessons schtarck un schee. (I do my lessons quickly and nicely.)

Susie/John: Mir gleiche die Schul. (We like school.) Mir dien gut Arwet. (We do good work.)

Aunt Lill (to all who are studying this lesson):

Dihr schtudiet alle Daag.
(You study every day.)
Dihr dient alles recht.
(You do everything right.)
Dihr dient schee Arwet.
(You do nice work.)

Er geht zu die Schul.

Phonics Tip

The "g" or "gg" in the middle of a word is really odd. The sound is almost a "w" or "y" sound.[13]

Examples:

Daage - say "daawe" (days)   Waage - say "vaawe" (wagon)   Regge - say "reye" (rain)

Grammar Tip

If someone says a negative statement (a sentence with the word "not"), do not answer "ya" (yes), but answer "yo," which is like saying "Yes, indeed!"

Examples:

"Dihr hent net en Dachweggeli." (*You have not a buggy*. You don't have a buggy.)

Answer: "Yo, mir hen en Dachweggeli." (Yes, we have a buggy.)

"Du gleischt net gschtampti Grummbiere." (*You like not mashed potatoes*. You don't like mashed potatoes.)

Answer: "Yo, ich gleich gschtampti Grummbiere." (Yes, I like mashed potatoes.)

Sie dien ihre Lessons an die Schul.

Ich gleich ihre Scooters.

Exercises

A. Use the verb chart to fill in the correct form of the verb "duh."

1. Sie (she) ___________ schee Arwet.
2. Dihr ___________ gut Arwet.
3. Sie (they) ___________ die Bicher.
4. Du ___________ alles recht.
5. Mir ___________ schlappich Arwet.
6. Er ___________ net gut Arwet.
7. Ich ___________ es recht.

B. Translate the sentences in A.

Culture Tip

A typical school day has four periods: two before lunch and two after lunch. Lunch and recess is one hour. Students who live close to school will go home for lunch, and then they will rush back in time to play.

In most Amish schools, all the students from first to eighth grade are in one room. Everything is done in order of age. When the teacher does roll call in the morning, she will do it in order of age. When the third graders come up for class, they come up in order of age and line up in order of age. This takes care of any cliques!

(die) Biewel

[p] Biewele

Bible

sachde

quiet+

quietly

(die) Schtori

[p] Schtories

story

laut

loud

loudly

aloud

(es) Wart

[p] Warte

word

letz

wrong

incorrectly+

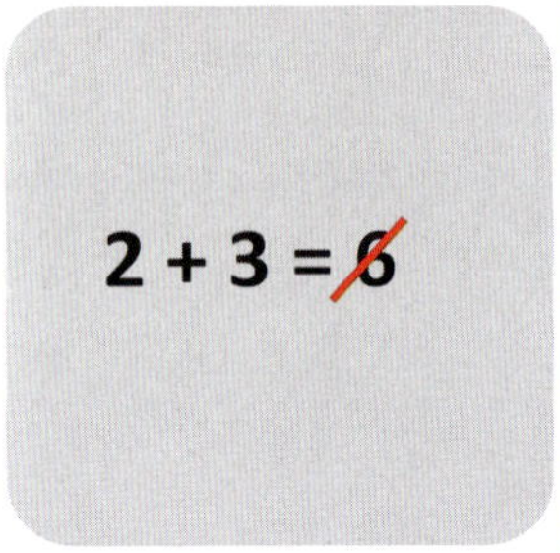

mariyets

in the morning

Verb	
lese (to read)	
ich	lees
du	lee**scht**
er, sie, es	lees**t**
mir	lese
dihr	lese**t**
sie	lese

Other Word	
an	at

Possessive Pronouns							
mei	**dei**	**sei**	**ihre**	**sei**	**unser**	**eier**	**ihre**
my	your [s]	his	her	its	our	your [p]	their

Lesson 9 - Reading at School

John: Die Becky is unser Teacher**.** (Becky is our teacher.)

Susie: Sie iss en gudi Teacher**.** (She is a good teacher.) Sie iss freindlich un schee. (She is friendly and nice.)

John: Mariyets leest sie die Biewel. (*In the morning reads she the Bible*. In the morning she reads the Bible.)

Susie: Mir lese en lot in die Schul. (We read a lot in school.)

John: Ich lees mei Lessons sachde an mei Desk**.** (I read my lessons quietly at my desk.)

Die Kinner lese ihre Schtories laut zu die Teacher**.** (The children read their stories aloud to the teacher.)

Susie: Die Mary Ann leest allfatt ihre Warte recht. (*The Mary Ann reads always her words correctly*. Mary Ann always reads her words correctly.)

John: Ebmols leest Der Davy sei Warte letz. (*Sometimes reads the Davy his words incorrectly*. Sometimes Davy reads his words incorrectly.)

Susie: John, du leescht dei Warte recht. (John, you read your words correctly.)

John: Ya, ich lees mei Warte recht. (Yes, I read my words correctly.)

Susie: Ich lees Library Bicher alle Daag. (I read library books every day.) Es iss Schpass. (It is fun.)

Aunt Lill (to all who are studying this lesson):

Leset dihr en lot Bicher? (*Read you a lot books?* Do you read a lot of books?)

Sin eier Bicher interesting? (Are your books interesting?)

Sie leest an ihre Desk.

Phonics Tip

I call the "ei" and "ie" Amish twins. When they are together, the *first* one is always quiet, and the *second* one speaks.[14] That means "ie" has the long "e" sound as in beet or meet, and "ei" has the long "i" sound as in bike or kite.

Examples:

s**ei** (his) - say sigh	Z**ei**t (time) - say tsight
d**ie** (the) - say dee	K**ie**h (cows) - say kee

Grammar Tips

Most Pennsylvania German-speaking people have never studied Pennsylvania German grammar in their life. They have learned it by hearing it, and so can you. If you think grammar is like eating dry bread, just ignore the grammar tips for this lesson and listen to the CD instead.

When an adjective (describing word) comes right before a **singular** noun (a noun that is only one), it has to agree with the noun. We call this "gender agreement." Here are the rules:

For a feminine noun, add "i" to the adjective.[15]

For a masculine noun, add "er" to the adjective.[16]

For a neuter noun, add nothing to the adjective.[17]

Spelling tip: When adding the "er" or "i" ending to an adjective that ends with a "t," change the "t" to a "d."[18]

Examples:

"Es iss en *gross**er*** Kuche." (It is a big cake.) "Kuche" is masculine, so add "er."

"Sie hen en *gross**i*** Biewel." (They have a big Bible.) "Biewel" is feminine, so add "i."

"Er iss en *gu**der*** Teacher." (He is a good teacher.) Here the teacher is a man (masculine), so add "er."

"Sell iss en *gu**der*** Boi." (That is a good pie.) "Boi" is masculine, so add "er."

"Ich hab en *glee* Buch." (I have a little book.) "Buch" is neuter, so do not add anything.

Die Scooters sin an die Schul.

When adding the "er" or "i" ending to an adjective like "glee" that ends with an "e," add an "n" to the adjective.[19]

Examples:

"Mir hen en *glee**ner*** Gaarde." (We have a little garden.)

"Ich hab en *schee**ni*** Biewel." (I have a pretty Bible.)

There are several exceptions to the above rules. One of them is: **When using the word *"der"* or *"die"* (the) before an adjective that precedes a *singular* noun, do not add any ending at all to the adjective!**[20] (See Lesson 24 for another exception.)

Examples:

"Ich gleich *der* **glee** Gaarde." (I like the little garden.)

"*Die* **gut** Teacher leest die Biewel mariyets." (The good teacher reads the Bible in the mornings.)

Culture Tip

At an Amish school, the first thing the Teacher does every morning is read from the Bible. Then everyone recites the Lord's Prayer together. After that, all the students line up in front of the school in order of age and sing three to four songs.

Sometimes a mom needs a babysitter, so she will send her four or five-year-old to school, and he/she will sit beside an older brother or sister for the day. The desks usually have wide seats so the younger sibling can easily fit.

If their homework is finished, the students are allowed to read library books. The seventh and eighth grade boys might even go outside and mow the school yard during school hours!

Exercises

A. Put the right ending on the adjectives in the following sentences. The first one is done for you.

1. Er iss en schmaert**er** Bauwer.
2. Mir hen en gross__ Buch.
3. Sie hen en laut___ Maschien.
4. Du hoscht en laut__ Gaul.
5. Es iss en glee___ Appel.
6. Dihr gleichet en gross__ Licht.
7. Ich gleich en schee____ Dachweggeli.

(der) Bu [p] Buwe boy		(es) Zeit [p] Zeite time	
(es) Maedel [p] Maed girl		vier four	
(die) Dallbopp [p] Dallbobbe doll		demiedich humble	
(der) Balle ball		grossfiehlich conceited	

Verb	
schpiele (to play)	
ich	schpiel
du	schpiel**scht**
er, sie, es	schpiel**t**
mir	schpiel**e**
dihr	schpiel**et**
sie	schpiel**e**

Other Words	
schpeeder	later
des, daer, die *	this

*See Lesson 24 for a more complete explanation of “des,” “daer,” and “die.”

“Grossfiehlich” literally means “big feeling.” Amish children are taught they should not brag. Of course, when their parents are not around, you might hear them bragging!

Lesson 10 - Recess

Susie: Nau iss es Zeit far Recess. (*Now is it time for recess*. Now it is time for recess.)

Die vier gleeni Maed schpiele Jump Rope. (The four little girls play jump rope.)

Schpeeder schpiele sie mit ihre Dallbobbe. (*Later play they with their dolls.* Later they play with their dolls.)

John: Die grossi Kinner un die Buwe schpiele Balle. (The big children and the boys play ball.)

Mir schpiele alle Daag. (We play every day.)

Susie: Ich gleich des. (I like this.)

Es iss Schpass! (It is fun.)

John, du schpielscht Balle hatt. (John, you play ball hard.)

John: Ya, ich duh. (Yes, I do.)

Ich schpiel hatt, awwer der Davy schpielt really hatt. (I play hard, but Davy plays really hard.)

Er iss schtarck. (He is strong.)

Susie: Der Davy iss grossfiehlich. (*The Davy is conceited*. Davy is conceited.)

John: Er iss net grossfiehlich! Er iss demiedich. (He is not conceited! He is humble.)

Aunt Lill (to all who are studying this lesson):

Schpielet dihr in eier Schul? (*Play you in your school*? Do you play in your school?)

Sie schpiele an die Schul.

Phonics Tips

When "bb" comes in the middle of a word, it has the "p" sound.[21]

Example: Bobbli (baby) - say Boppli

When "dd" comes in the middle of a word, it has the soft "t" sound.[22]

Example: Bedder (beds) [Lesson 13] - say Better

Grammar Tips

In the last lesson we learned that the noun and adjective have to agree when the noun is singular. If the noun is *plural*, the rule is very easy:

If the noun is plural, add "i" to the adjective in every case - if the noun is masculine, neuter, or feminine.

Examples:

Sell sin *gud**i*** Boi. (Those are good pies.)

Mir hen acht *gross**i*** Hinkel. (We have eight big chickens.)

Just like the last lesson**, if the adjective (describing word) ends with a vowel (a, e, i, o, or u), add "n" to the adjective before you add the ending.**[23]

Examples:

Ich hab siwwe *glee**ni*** Bicher. (I have seven little books.)

Dihr hent *schee**ni*** Kieh. (You have nice cows.)

Sie schpiele Balle.

Culture Tip

Children at Amish schools play softball for recess when the weather is favorable. Sometimes the younger children will play their own baseball game or another game on the other side of the school house.

All Amish boys have to wear a hat on the way to school. When it is cold, they might wear a stocking cap. At recess there is a lot of peer pressure to not wear a hat. Often only the more conservative boys or the preachers' boys will wear a hat, and sometimes even they will try to get by with not wearing one.

Baseball gloves are considered too worldly. Some of the boys wear batting gloves on both hands so the ball does not sting so much when they try to catch it. Once a year, the teacher and the 7th and 8th graders will visit another school for the day. At recess, they will play baseball against that school's 7th and 8th graders.

Exercises

A. Use the verb chart to fill in the correct form of the verb "schpiel."

1. Du ___________ mit en gleener Gaul.
2. Mir ____________ zammer.
3. Dihr ____________ balle in die Schul.
4. Sie (she) ____________ mit die Dollbopp.
5. Er ____________ mit der John.
6. Ich ____________ mit die Kinner.
7. Sie (they) ____________ in der Dreck.

B. Review! Change the following sentences by putting the word in bold print at the beginning. Make sure you change the noun and the pronoun correctly.

1. Sie schpiele mit unser Dollboppe **ebmols.**

____

2. Ich schpiel **allfatt** mit die Susie.

____

3. Er schpielt mit die Kinner **ebmols**.

____

(es) Babier [p] Babiere paper		(der) Freind friend	
(der) Pickder [p] Pickders picture		weiss white	
(der) Brief [p] Briefe letter		schusslich carelessly in a hurry	

Verb	
schreiwe (to write)	
ich	schreib
du	schreib**scht**
er, sie, es	schreib**t**
mir	schreiw**e**
dihr	schreiw**et**
sie	schreiw**e**

Other Words	
als	usually
nie net	never
nee	no
uff	on, up

Lesson 11 - Writing

Susie: Ich gleich schreiwe. (I like to write.)

Ich schreib en Brief zu mei Freind Lena in Honey Brook. (I write a letter to my friend Lena in Honey Brook.)

Ich schreib uff weiss Babier. (I write on white paper.)

John: Dei Babier hot scheeni Pickders. (Your paper has pretty pictures.)

Susie: Die Maem schreibt ebmols far *Die Botschaft*, awwer der Daett dutt nie net. (*The Mom writes sometimes for* Die Botschaft*, but the Dad does never*. Mom sometimes writes for *Die Botschaft*, but Dad never does.)

Er schreibt in der Circle Brief. (He writes in the circle letter.)

John: Schreibscht du in der Circle Brief? (*Write you in the circle letter?* Do you write in the circle letter?)

Susie: Nee, ich duh net! (No, I do not!)

Ich gleich net der Circle Brief. (*I like not the circle letter.* I don't like the circle letter.)

Die Uncles un die Aunts schreiwe als schlappich. (*The uncles and the aunts write usually sloppily.* The Uncles and Aunts usually write sloppily.)

John: Ya, ihre Warte sin letz. (Yes, their words are wrong.)

Ihre Schtories sin boring. (Their stories are boring.)

Susie: Sie sin zu schusslich.* (They are too careless.)

Aunt Lill (to all who are studying this lesson):

Schreiwet dihr Briefe zu eier Cousins? (*Write you letters to your cousins?* Do you write letters to your cousins?)

*The word "schusslich" is one of those amazing, difficult-to-translate words that make German so colorful. It means "working too fast, and in the meantime, doing a poor job and breaking things or tripping over things or spilling things." Being "schusslich" is definitely not being very efficient.

Der Circle Brief

Phonics Tip

The "v" has the "f" sound.[24] **Example:** vun (from) - say "funn"

Grammar Tip

When using two verbs in a simple sentence, the second verb is easy. Look at the word on the top of the word charts (the infinitive of the verb). That is the word used for the second verb.

Verb	
gleiche (to like)	
ich	gleich
du	gleich**scht**
er, sie, es	gleich**t**
mir	gleich**e**
dihr	gleich**et**
sie	gleich**e**

Verb	
schreiwe (to write)	
ich	schreib
du	schreib**scht**
er, sie	schreib**t**
mir	schreiw**e**
dihr	schreiw**et**
sie	schreiw**e**

Examples:

"Ich gleich **schreiwe**." (I like to write.)

"Du gleichscht **schreiwe**." (You like to write.)

"Er gleicht **schreiwe**." (He likes to write.)

"Sie gleiche **schreiwe**." (They like to write.)

"Mir gleiche **schreiwe**." (We like to write.)

"Dihr gleichet **schreiwe**." (You like to write.)

Mei Freind Lena

Er schreibt net schlappich.

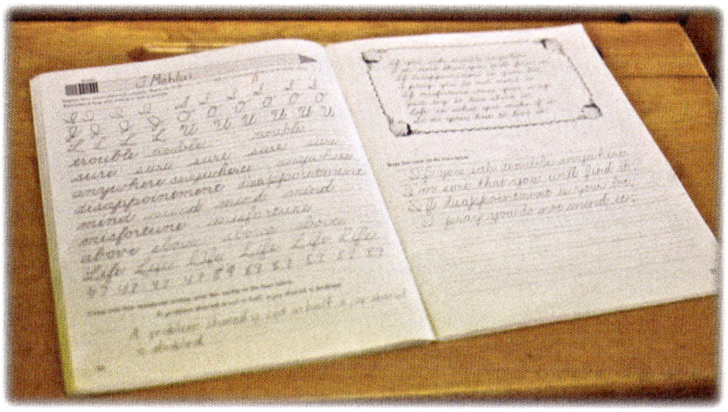

Exercises

A. Use the verb chart to fill in the correct form of the verb "schreiwe."

1. Ich ____________ zu die Susie.
2. Du ____________ an die Schul.
3. Sie (they) ____________ schlappich.
4. Sie (she) ____________ der Circle Brief.
5. Mir ____________ zammer.
6. Er ____________ mit en Pen.
7. Dihr ____________ alle Daag.

B. Make new sentences by adding another verb to these sentences. Remember to use the words from the top of the chart for the second verb.

1. Der John gleicht ______________.
2. Mir dien____________ alle Daag.
3. Sie (she) dutt ____________ mit die Dollbopp.
4. Ich gleich ____________ in es Haus.
5. Dihr dient ____________ an die Schul.

Culture Tips

Many Amish subscribe to a weekly newspaper, *Die Botschaft*, which has news from Amish communities all over the United States.

A lot of extended Amish families use circle letters to keep track of what is happening in each other's lives. One family will write a letter and send it to the next family. That family will add their own letter and send the pack to the next family, who will add their own letter, and so on. When the original family gets the pack, they will take out their old letter and add a new one. In our family's circle letter, the uncles' sloppy writing has become a family joke.

(der) Gut Mann

Gott

God

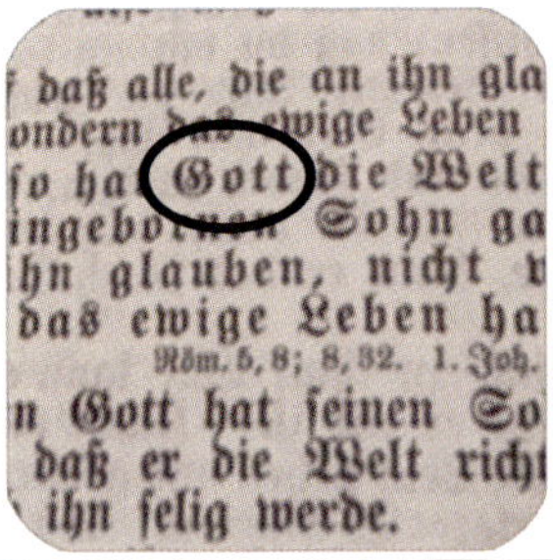

schpassich

funny

odd

(der) Dummkopp

[p] Dummkepp

dunce

wiescht

bad

ugly

Verb	
sehne (to see)	
ich	sehn
du	sehn**scht**
er, sie, es	sehn**t**
mir	sehn**e**
dihr	sehn**et**
sie	sehn**e**

Other Words	
anner	other
vun	of, from

Object Pronouns

mich	**dich**	**ihn**	**sie**	**es**	**uns**	**eich**	**sie**
me	you [s]	him	her	it	us	you [p]	them

Lesson 12 – School Happenings

John: Die Susie iss als gut in die Schul. (Susie is usually good in school.)

Ich sehn sie. (I see her.)

Susie: Ebmols sin die Buwe wiescht. (*Sometimes are the boys bad.* Sometimes the boys are bad.)

Sie schreiwe Notes zu en anner. (*They write notes to an other.* They write notes to each other.) Ich sehn sie. (I see them.)

John: Die Teacher sehnt sie net, awwer Der Gut Mann sehnt sie. (*The teacher sees them not, but the God sees them*. The teacher does not see them, but God sees them.)

Susie: John, der Davy schreibt ebmols Notes zu dich. *(John, the Davy writes sometimes notes to you*. John, sometimes Davy writes notes to you.)

John: Ya, er schreibt Notes zu mich, awwer ich bin ken Dummkopp*. (Yes, he writes notes to me, but I am no dunce.)

Ich schreib net Notes zu ihn! (*I write not notes to him!* I don't write notes to him.)

Susie: John, sehnscht du die Tourists? (*John, see you the tourists?* John, do you see the tourists?)

John: Ya, ich duh. (Yes, I do.) Sie sin schpassich*. (They are funny.)

Susie: Die Tourists sehne uns schpiele. (The tourists see us play.)

Aunt Lill (to all who are studying this lesson):

Dihr sehnet die Amishi Kinner.

(You see the Amish children.)

Sie sehne eich. (They see you.)

Der Davy

*"Dummkopp" is literally "dumb head" and describes a person with little common sense. John is not a "Dummkopp" because he knows that if he writes notes in school, he could get caught. He is too smart to get into trouble!

*"Schpassich" is used mostly to mean "odd." Speakers often use the loan word "funny" instead of "schpassich."

Phonics Tip

The "z" has the "ts" sound.[25] **Sometimes the "tz" has the "ts" sound as well.**[26]

Examples:

Zeit (time) - say "Tseit"   letz (wrong) - say "lets"

Grammar Tip

The object pronouns are used exactly as the object pronouns in English. Copy the object pronouns chart and place it to the right side of the subject pronouns chart.

Just as in English, most of the time the subject pronouns are used at the beginning of the sentence and the object pronouns at the end of the sentence.

Grammar experts: Object pronouns are used as objects of the preposition or as direct objects.

Examples:

Die Susie gleicht **mich**. (Susie likes me.)

Der Daett sehnt **uns**. (Dad sees us.)

All die Kinner sin Amish.

Die Tourists sehne uns.

Exercises

A. Use the verb chart to fill in the correct form of the verb "sehne."

1. Er ____________ die Maschien.
2. Du ____________ all die Eppel.
3. Sie (she) ____________ die gleeni Kinner.
4. Ich ____________ die schlappich Arwet.
5. Mir ____________ die Kieh.
6. Sie (they) ____________ unser Hinkel.
7. Dihr ____________ ihre Dachweggeli.

B. Translate the sentences in A.

Culture Tips

The words "Der Gut Mann" is used mostly when speaking to children. Literally, it means "The Good Man." Some families would not use that title because they would consider it disrespectful; God is more than just a man. However, it is used frequently, especially in Lancaster County. The word "Gott" is the more formal name for God.

Amish children are taught at a young age that God sees them. That makes them very conscientious. I would trust an Amish child with my pocketbook.

Tourists are part of the landscape in Lancaster County. Because they bring in a lot of money and help the economy, Amish consider them a beneficial nuisance.

(der) Schpeicher upstairs		(der) Bruder [p] Brieder brother	
(die) Kammer downstairs bed-room used by the parents		(die) Schweschder [p] Schweschdere sister	
(es) Bett [p] Bedder bed		(es) Bobbli [p] Bobblin baby	
(die) Schtubb [p] Schtuwwe room		schpot late	
(die) Uhr [p] Uhre clock		frieh early	

Lesson 13 - Sleeping

John: Ich schlof in der Schpeicher in mei Schtubb. (I sleep upstairs in my room.)

Der Bruder Jake schloft aa in mei Schtubb. (*The brother Jake sleeps also in my room*. Brother Jake also sleeps in my room.)

Susie, du schlofscht in der Schpeicher in dei Schtubb. (*Susie, you sleep in the upstairs in your room.* Susie, you sleep upstairs in your room.)

Susie: Ya, ich duh. (Yes, I do.)

Ich gleich mei Bett. (I like my bed.)

Ich geh frieh in es Bett. (*I go early in the bed.* I go to bed early).

Ich geh in es Bett an acht Uhr. (*I go in the bed at eight o'clock.* I go to bed at eight o'clock.)

John: Die Maem un der Daett schlofe in die Kammer. (Mom and Dad sleep in the master bedroom.)

Susie: Die Schweschder Mary schloft in ihre Crib. (Sister Mary sleeps in her crib.)

Sie iss en Bobbli. (She is a baby.)

John: Die Kieh un die Geil schlofe in die Scheier. (The cows and the horses sleep in the barn.)

John/Susie: Mir schlofe all gut. (*We sleep all good.* We all sleep well.)

Aunt Lill (to all who are studying this lesson):

Schlofet dihr schpot mariyets? (*Sleep you late in the morning*? Do you sleep late in the morning?)

Verb	
schlofe (to sleep)	
ich	schlof
du	schlof**scht**
er, sie, es	schlof**t**
mir	schlof**e**
dihr	schlof**et**
sie	schlof**e**

Er schloft in es Bett.

Phonics Tip

The letter "h" is quiet when it follows a vowel.[27]

Examples:

frieh (early) - say "free"   Kieh (cows) - say "kee"

Grammar Tip

Time is stated by saying the number and then "Uhr" (clock).[28]

Examples:

"siwwe Uhr"	(seven o'clock)	"acht Uhr"	(eight o'clock)
"nein Uhr"	(nine o'clock)	"drei Uhr"	(three o'clock)

The "Gut Schtubb "is a special bedroom just for visitors.

Pretty china and dishes are on display as décor.

Des iss die gut Schtubb.

Sie schlofe in die Schtubb.

Exercise

Use the verb chart to fill in the correct form of the verb "schlofe."

1. Ich ____________ in es Bett.
2. Du ____________ net an die Schul.
3. Sie (she) ____________ mit es Bobbli.
4. Sie (they) ____________ gut.
5. Mir ____________ net mariyets.
6. Er ____________ in die Schtubb.
7. Dihr ____________ net in die Scheier.

B. Translate the sentences in A.

Culture Tip

Most Amish people have the master bedroom downstairs.

When I was a little girl, an "English" neighbor came to the door. "Where is your mother?" she asked.

Mom had given birth to my new brother a few days earlier and was in the bedroom resting. "She's in the Kammer," I answered politely in my best English.

Later the worried neighbor asked my Dad, "How is your wife? Is she still in the coma?"

(es) Hinkel chicken		sechs six	
(der) Haar hair		fimf five	
halwer half		zehe ten	
schtruwwlich uncombed			

Other Words

eb	before
nooch	after
bis	until

Verb

schteh (to stand)	
ich	schteh (schtehn ich)
du	schteh**scht**
er, sie, es	schteh**t**
mir	schtehn
dihr	schtehn**t**
sie	schtehn

Lesson 14 – Waking Up

Susie: Ich gleich uff schteh. (*I like up stand.* I like getting up.)

Ich schteh uff an sechs Uhr. (*I stand up at six hour*. I get up at six o'clock.)

John, du schtehscht aa frieh uff. (*John, you stand also early up*. John, you also get up early.)

John: Ya, ich duh, awwer ich gleich net frieh uff schteh. (*Yes, I do, but I like not early up stand*. Yes, I do, but I do not like to get up early.)

Susie: Mir dien all frieh uff schteh. (*We do all early up stand*. We all get up early.)

Mir schtehn uff eb die Sunn, awwer die Hinkel schtehn uff eb uns. (*We stand up before the sun, but the chickens stand up before us*. We get up before the sun, but the chickens get up before us.)

John: Der Daett un die Maem schtehn uff eb uns. (*The Dad and the Mom stand up before us*. Dad and Mom get up before us.)

Der Daett schteht uff an fimf Uhr. (*The Dad stands up at five hour*. Dad gets up at five o'clock.)

Er schafft in die Scheier eb Breakfast. (He works in the barn before breakfast.)

Susie: Die Maem schteht uff nooch der Daett. (Mom gets up after Dad.) Sie schteht uff an halwer sechs. (*She stands up at half six*. Mom gets up at five-thirty.)

Die Mary schteht schpot uff. (*The Mary stands late up*. Mary gets up late.)

Sie schloft bis zehe Uhr. (*She sleeps until ten hour*. She sleeps until ten o'clock.)

Sie iss en Bobbli. (She is a baby.)

John: Der Bruder Jake schteht aa schpot uff. (*The brother Jake stands also late up*. Brother Jake also gets up late.)

Er schloft bis halwer acht. (*He sleeps until half eight*. He sleeps until seven-thirty.) Er iss glee. (He is little.)

Susie, du bischt alles schtruwwlich mariyets. (*Susie, you are everything uncombed in the morning*. Susie, you are very uncombed in the morning.)

Susie: Ich bin net! (I am not!) Du bischt! (You are!)

Dei Haar sin schtruwwlich! (Your hair is uncombed!)

Aunt Lill (to all who are studying this lesson):

Schtehnt dihr frieh uff? (*Stand you early up*? Do you get up early?)

Phonics Tip

The letters "aa" have the "aw" sound.[29]

Examples:

aa (also) - say "aw" Haar (hair) - say "hawr" Yaahr (year) - say "yawr"

Grammar Tips

In Pennsylvania German, people do not "wake up" or "get up," they "stand up." A first grade Amish girl may say in English, "I stood up at six o'clock this morning." She is simply translating directly from Pennsylvania German.

To say "six-thirty" or "seven-thirty," **use the word "halwer" (half) and the *next* hour.**[30]

Examples:

"halwer siwwe" [half seven] (six-thirty) "halwer acht" [half eight] (seven-thirty)

In Lesson 11, we used the word on *top* of the verb chart for the second verb. Most of the other words that describe go *between* the two verbs. In the following examples, the verbs are in bold print (adverbs or adverb phrases that say "when" or "where" can come after the first *or* second verb, depending on the emphasis - see Lesson 22).

Examples:

Ich **gleich** uff **schteh**. (*I like up get*. I like to get up.)

Mir **dien** all frieh uff **schteh**. (*We do all early up get*. We all get up early.)

Ich **gleich** net frieh uff **schteh.** (*I like not early up get*. I do not like to get up early.)

Die Maem schteht frieh uff.

Es iss nein Uhr.

Exercises

A. Use the verb chart to fill in the correct form of the verb "schteh."

1. Dihr ____________ uff eb die Sunn.
2. Du ____________uff nooch mich.
3. Sie (they) ____________ schpot uff.
4. Er ____________ uff en Appel. Er iss schpassich.
5. Mir ____________ frieh uff.
6. Ich ____________ uff der Dreck.
7. Sie (she) ____________ frieh uff mariyets.

B. Translate the sentences in A.

Culture Tip

Amish people generally get up quite early, especially those who live on a farm. This is considered honorable. Very early in the morning, laundry is hanging on the wash lines - a symbol of the hard-working ladies who live there.

Soon after Dad was married, Grandpa came to the house early in the morning. He was surprised to see Dad and Uncle Davy already playing checkers.

"Wow, you're up early," he said approvingly. They kept playing checkers without saying a word. What Grandpa did not know is that they had been playing all night!

(es) Haus [p] Heiser house 	(die) Leit people 
(der) Schtuhl [p] Schtiel chair 	hesslich ugly terrible 
(der) Eckschank [p] Eckschenk corner cupboard 	dreckich dirty 
(es) Eck [p] Ecke corner 	pivvich particular 

Verb	
butze (to clean)	
ich	butz
du	butz**scht**
er, sie, es	butz**t**
mir	butz**e**
dihr	butz**et**
sie	butz**e**

Other Words	
yuscht	just
deel	some
unnich	under

Lesson 15 – Cleaning

Susie: Die Maem un ich butze es Haus heit. (Mom and I clean the house today.)

John: Ich gleich net butze. *(I like not to clean.* I don't like to clean.)

Susie: Ich duh! Ich gleich butze. (I do! I like to clean.)

John: Ok, du butzscht in es Haus, un ich schaff in die Scheier. (Ok, you clean in the house, and I work in the barn.)

Susie: Ya, geh! (Yes, go!) Butz die Scheier! (Clean the barn!)

*Es iss hesslich dreckich. (It is terribly dirty.)

John: *Es iss net! (It is not!)

Du bischt yuscht pivvich. (You are just particular.)

Susie: Die Maem butzt die Kich un ich butz die Sitz Schtubb. (Mom cleans the kitchen and I clean the sitting room.)

Ich butz alle eck. (I clean every corner.)

Ich butz unnich der Eckschank un unnich die Schtiehl. (I clean under the corner cupboard and under the chairs.)

Deel Leit butze net die Ecke. (*Some people clean not the corners*. Some people do not clean the corners.)

Sie sin net pivvich. (They are not particular.)

Aunt Lill (to all who are studying this lesson):

Butzet dihr eier Schtubb alle Daag?

(*Clean you your room every day?*

Do you clean your room every day?)

> Although "hesslich" means "ugly," native speakers often use it to mean "very" or "terribly."
>
> "Es iss hesslich gross."
>
> (It is very big.)
>
> "Der Gaul iss hesslich schtarck."
>
> (The horse is very fast.)

Die Scheier iss hesslich dreckich.

*Some speakers might say "Sie iss hesslich dreckich," and "Sie iss net" because "Scheier" is a feminine noun, and they are making the pronoun agree with the noun.

Phonics Tip

The letters "au" are almost like the "o" sound in "tot," but it is more drawn out. Listen to the CD for the correct pronunciation.

Example:

laut (loud)   Gaul (horse)

Grammar Tip

A command in Pennsylvania German is easy. Use the first verb on the chart to give a command to one person, and the fifth word on the chart to give a command to more than one person. (Exception: the verb "Sei" (to be): sei [one person] seint [more than one person])

Examples:

To one person: **Geh** zu die Schul. (Go to school.)

To more than one person: **Gehnt** zu die Schul. (Go to school.)

To one person: **Schpiel** schee. (Play nicely.)

To more than one person: **Schpielet** schee. (Play nicely.)

Verb	
geh (to go)	
⇨ ich	geh
du	geh**scht**
er, sie, es	geh**t**
mir	geh**n**
⇨ dihr	geh**nt**
sie	geh**n**

Verb	
schpiele (to play)	
⇨ ich	schpiel
du	schpiel**scht**
er, sie, es	schpiel**t**
mir	schpiel**e**
⇨ dihr	schpiel**et**
sie	schpiel**e**

Der Eckschank

Die Sitz Schtubb

Exercises

A. Use the verb chart to fill in the correct form of the verb "butze."

1. Dihr ____________ es Haus.
2. Du ____________ es Dachweggeli.
3. Er ____________ sei Maschien.
4. Sie (they) ____________ die Schul.
5. Mir ____________ unser Scheier.
6. Sie (she) ____________ ihre Schtubb.
7. Ich ____________ all die Ecke.

B. Translate the sentences in A.

Culture Tip

More old-fashioned Amish have a "Sitz Schtubb," which literally means "sitting room." This is a parlor where heirlooms and family records are kept. Often rag carpets cover the floor. The room is used only on Sunday for special guests. Both of my grandmothers had a Sitz Schtubb, but many of the younger generation do not.

The "Eckschank" is a corner cupboard for special china and keepsakes. My grandmother had a beautiful set of red china in hers. She never used it in her entire life, and one day I asked her why. She said she was afraid it would break!

(der) Kaes cheese		drauss outside	
(die) Millich milk		nein nine	
gehl yellow		gluschdich desirous rather than hungry for food	

Verb	
welle (to want)	
ich	will
du	wit**t**
er, sie, es	will
mir	well**e**
dihr	well**et**
sie	well**e**

Other Words	
meh	more
was	what
eppes	something
odder	or
nix	nothing

Lesson 16 – Hungry Before Dinner

John: Was Zeit iss es? (What time is it?)

Susie: Es iss nein Uhr. (*It is nine hour.* It is nine o'clock.)

John: Ich bin hungerich. (I am hungry.)

Susie: Du bischt net hungerich. (You are not hungry.) Du bischt yuscht gluschdich*. (You are just desiring food.)

John: Yo, ich bin hungerich. (Yes, I am hungry.) Ich will eppes far esse. (*I want something for to eat.* I want something to eat.)

Susie: Was witt? (*What want?* What do you want?) Kaes un Pretzels? (Cheese and pretzels?)

Odder Cookies un Millich? (Or cookies and milk?)

John: Ich will Kaes un Pretzels. (I want cheese and pretzels.)

Susie: Witt meh? (*Want more?* Do you want more?)

John: Nee, es iss genunk. (No, it is enough.)

Der Daett iss drauss. (Dad is outside.) Er will aa eppes. (*He wants also something*. He also wants something.)

Susie: Was will er? (*What wants he?* What does he want?)

John: Er will aa Kaes un Pretzels. (*He wants also cheese and pretzels*. He also wants cheese and pretzels.)

Ich will gehler Kaes, awwer er will weisser Kaes. (I want yellow cheese, but he wants white cheese.)

Susie: Sie welle allfatt eppes eb Dinner. (*They want always something before dinner.* They always want something before dinner.)

Die Maem will nix. (Mom wants nothing.) Sie iss net gluschdich. (She is not desiring food.)

Aunt Lill (to all who are studying this lesson):

Wellet dihr nau esse? (*Want you now to eat?* Do you want to eat now?)

*"Gluschdich" does not mean truly hungry, but "having a craving." If someone is "gluschdich" for chocolate, they are craving it even though they have just finished eating a huge meal of mashed potatoes and chicken.

Er will en Drink.

Phonics Tip

The letters "chs" have the "x" sound.[31]

Example:

sechs (six) - say "sex"

Grammar Tip

There are a few cases in Pennsylvania German where the pronoun can be dropped when it is understood. One such case is when one person is asked a question.

Examples:

"Was witt?" (What want?) **or** "Was witt du?" (*What want you?* What do you want?)

"Witt meh?" (Want more?) **or** "Witt du meh?" (*Want you more?* Do you want more?)

Culture Tip

On a farm, when the men are making hay or thrashing wheat, the women will bring a snack out to them about nine o'clock. Dinner is around eleven-thirty. Sometimes the men take a short dinner nap, but then they will go back to work again. At three o'clock, the women bring another snack. The men will work until five o'clock supper, and after supper they will work until sundown.

Exercises

A. Use the verb chart to fill in the correct form of the verb "welle."

1. Sie (they) ____________ fimf Bedder.
2. Sie (she) ____________ Eppelsaes.
3. Er ____________ en Kuh.
4. Dihr ____________ en grosser Gaul.
5. Mir ____________ en Uhr.
6. Du ____________ nein Grummbiere.
7. Ich ____________ en glee Hinkel.

B. Translate the sentences in A.

Sie welle eppes far esse.

(der) Hund [p] Hunde dog		(die) Blumm [p] Blumme flower	
(die) Schtadt [p] Schtedt city		(die) Bawwerei farm	
(die) Grossmammi grandmother		grie green+	
(der) Grossdaadi grandfather		sauwer clean	

Other Words	
weil	because
ganz	quite,+ all

Verb	
wuhne (to live)	
ich	wuhn
du	wuhn**scht**
er, sie, es	wuhn**t**
mir	wuhn**e**
dihr	wuhn**et**
sie	wuhn**e**

Lesson 17 – Where We Live

Susie: Ich wuhn in Leola. (I live in Leola.)

John/Susie: Mir wuhne uff en Bawwerei. (We live on a farm.)

Susie: Wuhnscht du drauss odder in es Haus? (*Live you outside or in the house?* Do you live outside or in the house?)

John: Ich wuhn in es Haus! (I live in the house!)

Yuscht die Kieh un die Geil wuhne drauss. (Only the cows and the horses live outside.)

Susie: Der Uncle Henry wunt in die Schtadt. (Uncle Henry lives in the city.)

John: Er hot en Maschien. (He has a car.)

Er iss net Amish. (He is not Amish.)

Susie: Der Uncle Henry sei Maschien iss grie. (*The Uncle Henry his car is green*. Uncle Henry's car is green.)

John: Er hot en Hund. (He has a dog.)

Susie: Ich gleich net sei Hund, weil er zu gross iss.* (*I like not his dog, because he too big is.* I do not like his dog, because he is too big.)

John: Ich gleich schpiele mit sei Hund. (I like to play with his dog.) Es iss Schpass. (It is fun.)

Susie: Der Grossdaadi un die Grossmammi wuhne in Gordonville. (Grandfather and Grandmother live in Gordonville.)

Ihre Haus iss ganz glee. (Their house is quite small.)

John: Sie hen gehli, roti, un blohi Blumme. (They have yellow, red and blue flowers.)

Susie: Ihre Haus iss allfatt sauwer. (Their house is always clean.)

Aunt Lill (to all who are studying this lesson):

Wuhnet dihr in die Schtadt? (*Live you in the city?* Do you live in the city?)

*See Lesson 18 for this sentence structure.

Die Nochbere wuhne uff en Bawwerei.

Phonics Tip

A vowel is short if -it is followed by more than one consonant.[32]

-it is followed by one consonant at the end of the word.[33]

The short "a" has the "o" sound as in "hop."[34]

Examples:

Warte (words) lang (long)

Grammar Tips

In Lesson 9, we learned possessive pronouns. To show ownership with a noun is different.

When something belongs to a woman, say her name and add "ihre":

"**Die Mary ihre** Haus iss schee." (*The Mary her house is nice.* Mary's house is nice.)

"**Die Susie ihre** Scooter iss glee." (*The Susie her scooter is little.* Susie's scooter is little.)

When something belongs to a man, say his name and add "sei":

"**Der Uncle Henry sei** Maschien iss grie." (*The Uncle Henry his car is green.* Uncle Henry's car is green.)

"**Der John sei** Scooter iss gross." (*The John his scooter is big.* John's scooter is big.)

When something belongs to a group, say the group's name and add "ihre":

"**Die Nochbere ihre** Dachweggeli iss sauwer." (*The neighbors their buggy is clean.* The neighbor's buggy is clean.)

"**Die Buwe ihre** Schtubb iss dreckich." (*The boys their room is dirty.* The boys' room is dirty.)

Der Daett sei Cousin Katie hot scheeni Blumme.

Die Leit wuhne in en gross Haus.

Exercise

A. Use the verb chart to fill in the correct form of the verb “wuhne.”

1. Dihr ____________ in Bird-in-Hand.
2. Du ____________ in die Country.
3. Sie (she) ____________ in en glee Haus.
4. Sie (they) ____________ uff en Bawwerei.
5. Mir ____________ net in die Scheier.
6. Er ____________ in die Schtadt.
7. Ich ____________ in en gross Haus.

B. Translate the following sentences into Pennsylvania German.

Mary’s house is pretty. ______________________________

John’s horse is big. ______________________________

The neighbors’ barn is clean. ______________________________

Culture Tip

Amish people do not live in the city. They live in towns or in rural areas. Their lawns and gardens are exceptionally well kept and beautiful.

My grandma’s house was always spotless and extremely neat.

(der) Disch table		voll full	
schwatz black		do here	
gschwindt quickly		datt there	

Verb	
kumme (to come)	
ich	kumm
du	kumm**scht**
er, sie, es	kumm**t**
mir	kumm**e**
dihr	kumm**et**
sie	kumm**e**

Other Words	
wann	when
mariye	tomorrow
ferwas	why
glei	soon

Lesson 18 – Visitors

John: The Grossdaadi un die Grossmammi kumme mariye. (Grandfather and Grandmother come tomorrow.)

Sie kumme mit ihre schwatzer Gaul. (They come with their black horse.)

Susie: Gut! (Good!)

Ich gleich wann sie kumme. (I like when they come.)

John: Datt kummt der Jake. (There comes Jake.)

Er iss unser Cousin. (*He is our cousin.* He is our cousin.)

Susie: Hi, Jake. Ferwas kummscht du? (*Why come you*? Why do you come?)

Jake: Ich kumm weil ich will do esse. (*I come because I want here to eat.* I come because I want to eat here.)

Susie: Gut! (Good!) Supper iss glei ready. (Supper is soon ready.)

Maem: Kummet esse! (Come eat!) Supper iss ready. (Supper is ready.)

Susie: Mir kumme gschwindt weil mir hungerich sin. (*We come quickly because we hungry are.* We come quickly because we are hungry.)

Jake: Der Disch iss ganz voll vun Ess-sach! (The table is quite full of food.)

Ich gleich esse. (I like to eat).

Aunt Lill (to all who are studying this lesson):

Kummet dihr zu die Schul? (*Come you to the school?* Do you come to school?)

Sie kummt mit ihre Gaul.

Sie kumme all zammer.

Phonics Tip

Remember, a vowel is short if

-it is followed by more than one consonant.[35]
-it is followed by one consonant at the end of the word.[36]

The short "e" has the "e" sound as in "ten."[37]

Examples: fett (fat) Ess-sach (food)

Grammar Tip

In compound sentences with the conjunctions (connecting words) "un" (and), "awwer" (but), or "odder" (or), each half of the sentence has the normal word order.[38]

However, in sentences with subordinating conjunctions like "weil" (because), "wann" (when), or "eb" (before), the second part of the sentence is more tricky; in most cases, the verb comes at the *end* of that phrase.[39] In other words, the second verb box is split in half!

Examples: **Mir kumme gschwindt** weil **mir hungerich sin.** (*We come quickly because we hungry are.* We come quickly because we are hungry.)

Verb	
kumme (to come)	
ich	kumm
du	kumm**scht**
er, sie	kumm**t**
mir	kumm**e**
dihr	kumm**et**
sie	kumm**e**

gschwindt ***weil***

Verb
sei (to be)
ich
du
er, sie
mir
dihr
sie

hungerich

bin
bi**scht**
iss
sin
sint
sin

Exercises

A. Use the verb chart to fill in the correct form of the verb "kumme."

1. Dihr ____________ eb Breakfast.
2. Er ____________ far Supper.
3. Sie (they) ____________ zu unser Haus.
4. Ich ____________ mit en Dachweggeli.
5. Mir ____________ mit en Gaul.
6. Sie (she) ____________ mariye.
7. Du ____________ zu die Gmee.

B. Translate the sentences in A.

Sie kumme mit Scooters.

Culture Tip

On Saturday, Amish women often make extra dessert and bread, because relatives or friends might drop by uninvited on Sunday. This is not considered rude. During the week this may happen as well, but it is more likely on Sunday.

(es) Brot

bread

eens

one

(es) Hoi

hay

zwee

two

(die) Gwilt

[p] Gwilts

quilts

waarm

warm

(der) Leeb

loaf

verleedt

discouraged

(es) Wedder

weather

Other Words	
deel	some [+]

Verb	
mache (to make)	
ich	mach
du	mach**scht**
er, sie, es	mach**t**
mir	mach**e**
dihr	mach**et**
sie	mach**e**

Lesson 19 – Making Things

Susie: Heit mach ich Cookies. (*Today make I cookies*. Today I make cookies.)

John: Mariye machscht Kuche. (*Tomorrow make cake.* Tomorrow you make cake.)

Die Maem macht weiss Brot. (Mom makes white bread.)

Susie: Sie macht zwee Leeb - eens far uns un eens far die Nochbere. (She makes two loaves - one for us and one for the neighbors.)

Die Maem un die Grossmammi mache deel Gwilts. (Mom and Grandmother make some quilts.)

John: Die Gwilts sin grie un purple un rot un bloh. (The quilts are green and purple and red and blue.)

Susie: Sie sin schee. (They are pretty.)

John: Susie, machscht du aa Gwilts? (*Susie, make you also quilts?* Susie, do you also make quilts?)

Susie: Ya, ich duh. (Yes, I do.)

(Later John and Dad are working out in the field.)

John: Es Wedder iss waarm heit. (The weather is warm today.)

Der Daett un ich mache Hoi. (Dad and I make hay.)

Mir schaffe hatt. (We work hard.)

Mir hen en lot Hoi. (*We have a lot hay.* We have a lot of hay.)

Ich will net schaffe. (I want not to work. I do not want to work.)

Ich bin verleedt*. (I am discouraged.)

Aunt Lill (to all who are studying this lesson):

Machet dihr Brot? (*Make you bread?* Do you make bread?)

*People use "verleedt" in relation to work that will take a long time or a lot of effort, or to a difficult situation. "I dread doing this," may be a more accurate translation for "Ich bin verleedt."

Er macht Hoi mit der Daed.

Phonics Tip

Remember, a vowel is short if -it is followed by more than one consonant.[40]

-it is followed by one consonant at the end of the word.[41]

The short "i" has the "i" sound as in "big."[42]

Examples: dinn (thin) fimf (five)

Grammar Tip

We learned in Lesson 16 that you can drop the pronoun when you are asking one person a question. **The pronoun can also be dropped when talking directly to someone *and* they have already been addressed as "du" in a sentence before *and* it is preceded by an adverb.**

Examples:

John: Du machscht en lot Cookies heit. (*You make a lot cookies today.* You make a lot of cookies today.)

John: *Mariye* machscht meh. (*Tomorrow make more.* Tomorrow you make more.)

The pronoun may also be dropped if *they* have been talking about themselves before.

Examples:

Susie: Heit mach ich Cookies. (*Today make I cookies.* Today I make cookies.)

John: Mariye machscht Kuche. (*Tomorrow make cake.* Tomorrow you make cake.)

Culture Tip

Oh my, John is complaining about work. That is very unusual for Amish children. An Amish boy who complains about work is admitting that he is a sissy. He is lazy. Being considered lazy is a **huge** insult.

Exercises

A. Use the verb chart to fill in the correct form of the verb "mache."

1. Dihr ____________ scheeni Gwilts.
2. Mir ____________ gschtampti Grummbiere far Dinner.
3. Er ____________ Dachweggelin.
4. Sie (they) ___________ Kaes mit Millich.
5. Du ____________ Eppel Boi far Supper.
6. Sie (she) ____________ Eppelsaes mit ihre Kinner.
7. Ich ____________ en Leeb Brot.

B. Translate the sentences in A.

Sie macht Boi far die Gmee.

(der) Mann

[p] Mannsleit

man

kalt

cold

(die) Weibsleit

women

froh

happy

glad

(die) Gleeder

clothing

reich

rich

(es) Geld

money

aarm

poor

(es) Wexel

change

Other Words	
blendi	plenty

Verb	
gewwe (to give)	
ich	geb
du	geb**scht**
er, sie, es	geb**t**
mir	geww**e**
dihr	geww**et**
sie	geww**e**

Lesson 20 – Giving to the Poor

Susie: Die Weibsleit gewwe Gwilts zu die aarmi Leit. (The women give quilts to the poor people.)

John: Die aarmi Leit sin froh far die Gwilts wann es kalt iss Drauss. (*The poor people are happy for the quilts when it cold is outside.* The poor people are happy for the quilts when it is cold outside.)

Der Dactt gebt sie Geld. (Dad gives them money.)

Susie: Ich geb Wexel vun mei Piggy Bank. (I give change from my piggy bank.)

John, gebscht du Geld zu die aarmi Leit? (*John, give you money to the poor people?* John, do you give money to the poor people?)

John: Ya, ich duh. (Yes, I do.)

Ich bin net reich, awwer ich hob blendi. (I am not rich, but I have plenty.)

Ich gleich gewwe. (I like to give.)

Susie: Ebmols gewwe mir Fleesch. (*Sometimes give we meat.* Sometimes we give meat.)

Deel Leit gewwe Gleeder. (Some people give clothing.)

Die Grossmammi gebt Biewele. (Grandmother gives Bibles.)

John: Die Mannsleit mache Heiser. (The men make houses.)

Sie schaffe hatt.

(They work hard.)

Aunt Lill (to all who are studying this lesson):

Gewwet dihr Geld zu die aarmi Leit?

(*Give you money to the poor people?*

Do you give money to the poor people?)

Die Weibsleit gewwe Gwilts zu die aarmi Leit.

Sie gebt Gwilts zu die aarmi Leit.

Phonics Tip:

Remember, a vowel is short if

-it is followed by more than one consonant.[43]
-it is followed by one consonant at the end of the word.[44]

The short "o" is like the "u" sound in "cut."[45] Listen to the CD for the correct pronunciation.

Examples:

hot (have)   Bobbli (baby)

Some words with "o" that follow the rules for short vowels have the long "o" sound. See Lesson 25.

Grammar Tip:

In Lesson 12, we used the object pronouns as direct objects.

Examples: Ich sehn **sie**. (I see her.)

Sie gleiche **uns**. (They like us.)

Object pronouns can also be used as indirect objects, just as in English.

Examples: Der Daett gebt **sie** Geld. (Dad gives them money.)

Ich geb **ihn** en Biewel. (I give him a Bible.)

Object pronouns can also be used as objects of the preposition, just as in English.

Examples: Mir gewwe Geld zu **sie**. (We give money to them.)

Du gebscht Geld zu **mich**. (You give money to me.)

Culture Tip

Many Amish women make quilts or blankets for poor people in other countries. The Amish are huge contributors of Christian Aid Ministries, a conservative charity that distributes funds and goods to needy people all over the world.

The Amish are very active in rebuilding after disasters. Whole busloads of Amish will descend on an area and get to work. The women do the cooking and help with the cleanup, and the men rebuild. Amish people get an amazing amount of work done in a short period of time.

Exercises

A. Use the verb chart to fill in the correct form of the verb "gewwe."

1. Sie (she) ____________ es Bobbli Millich.
2. Ich ____________ ihn en Leeb Brot.
3. Er____________ Kieh zu die aarmi Leit.
4. Dihr ____________ die Kinner en Cookie.
5. Sie (they) ____________ uns Wexel.
6. Mir ____________ sie Shoo-fly Boi.
7. Du ____________ Geld zu der Mann.

B. Translate the sentences in A.

Die Mannsleit mache en Scheier.

(der) Voggel

[p] Veggel

bird

drei

three

(der) Blatz

[p] Bletz

place

brau

brown

(die) Gans

[p] Gens

goose

neegscht

near

close

(die) Wutz

[p] Wutze

pig

weit

far

(der) Schof

sheep

Other Words	
wu	where

Verb	
laafe (to walk)	
ich	laaf
du	laaf**scht**
er, sie, es	laaf**t**
mir	laaf**e**
dihr	laaf**et**
sie	laaf**e**

Lesson 21 – Walking to Church

Susie: Heit iss die Gmee. (Today is church.)

Mir laafe zu die Gmee weil es neegscht iss. (*We walk to the church because it near is*. We walk to church because it is near.)

John: Wu iss die Gmee? (Where is church?)

Susie: Die Gmee iss an es Dans ihre Blatz. (*The church is at the Dans their place.* The church is at Dans' place.) Sie sin unser Nochbere. (They are our neighbors.)

John: Ich laaf zu die Gmee mit dich. (I walk to church with you.)

Die Maem laaft mit der Daett. (Mom walks with Dad.)

Sie laafe langsam. (They walk slowly.)

Susie: Ich gleich laafe mit dich. (I like to walk with you.)

Du laafscht schtarck. (You walk fast.)

John: Datt sin drei brauni Veggel. (There are three brown birds.)

Susie: Un datt sin deel Gens. (And there are some geese.)

John: Datt sin deel dreckichi Wutze. (There are some dirty pigs.)

Susie: Datt sin deel Schof. (There are some sheep.) Sie sin sauwer. (They are clean.)

John: Nau sin mir an die Gmee. (Now we are at church.)

Susie: Datt kummt es Mervins ihre Dachweggeli. (*There comes the Mervins their buggy.* There comes Mervins' buggy.)

John: Sie wuhne weit vun do. (They live far from here.)

Aunt Lill (to all who are studying this lesson):

Laafet dihr zu die Gmee? (*Walk you to the church?* Do you walk to church?)

Sie laafe zu die Gmee.

Sie laafe vun die Gmee.

Phonics Tip

Remember, a vowel is short if

-it is followed by more than one consonant.[46]
-it is followed by one consonant at the end of the word.[47]

The short "u" is like the "oo" sound in book."[48]

Examples: dumm (stupid) Schtubb (room)

Grammar Tip

Use the word "es" when referring to a whole family.

Amish people generally refer to a whole family by the father's name. "Es Dans" means Dan and his wife and their children. Even though "Dans" is plural (more than one), use the word "es."

Examples:

"Mir gehn zu es Dans ihre Blatz." (*We go to the Dans their place.* We go to Dans' place.)

"Es Uncle Henrys sin do." (*The Uncle Henrys are here.* Uncle Henrys are here.)

Culture Tip

The Amish have church every other Sunday. Instead of having a church house, they meet in each other's homes. Their churches are divided into districts geographically. From twenty to forty families live in each district. On the "off" Sunday, families might visit another Amish church or visit relatives and friends.

Exercises

A. Use the verb chart to fill in the correct form of the verb "laafe."

1. Er ____________ schtarck.
2. Du ____________ langsam.
3. Sie (she) ____________ mit ihn.
4. Dihr ____________ weil ihre blatz neegscht iss.
5. Ich ____________ zu die Nochbere.
6. Mir ____________ zu die Schul.
7. Sie (they) ____________ mit uns.

B. Translate the sentences in A.

Die Gmee iss do heit.

(die) Bank
[p] Benk
bench

gawwerich
standing or sitting in an awkward position

(der) Breddicher
preacher

schtill
still

(der) Schockel-schtuhl
[p] Schockelschtiehl
chair

unruhich
restless

(es) Schnuppduch
[p] Schnuppdicher
handkerchief

griddlich
cranky

lang
long

Verb	
hocke (to sit)	
ich	hock
du	hock**scht**
er, sie, es	hock**t**
mir	hock**e**
dihr	hock**et**
sie	hock**e**

Other Words	
midd	middle

Lesson 22 – Sitting in Church

John: In die Gmee hock ich uff en Bank mit die grossi Buwe. (*In the church sit I on a bench with the big boys.* In church I sit on a bench with the big boys.)

Susie, du hockscht mit die Maem. (Susie, you sit with Mom.)

Susie: Ya, ich will mit die Maem hocke an die Gmee. (*Yes, I want with the Mom to sit at the church.* Yes, I want to sit with Mom at church.)

Ich hock net mit die grossi Maed. (*I sit not with the big girls.* I do not sit with the big girls.) Ich bin zu glee. (I am too little.)

John: Die Grossmammi hockt uff un Schockelschtul weil sie alt iss. (*Grandmother sits on a rocking chair because she old is*. Grandmother sits on a rocking chair because she is old.)

Susie: Unser Gmee hot fier Breddicher. (Our church has four preachers.)

Sie hocke in die Midd. (They sit in the middle.)

John: Die Gmee iss als lang. (The church is usually long.)

Susie: Mir hocke un hocke un hocke un hocke. (We sit and sit and sit and sit.)

John: Die gleeni Kinner sin als unruhich. (The little children are usually restless.)

Susie: Die Bobblin sin griddlich. (The babies are cranky.)

John: Susie, du hockscht net schtill in die Gmee. (*Susie, you sit not still in the church.* Susie, you do not sit still in church.)

Du bischt gawwerich. (You are sitting awkwardly.)

Susie: Ich bin net gawwerich! (I am not sitting awkwardly!) Ich hock schtill. (I sit still.)

Ich schpiel mit mei Schnuppduch. (I play with my handkerchief.)

John: Die Susie macht gleeni Bobblin mit ihre Schnuppduch. (Susie makes little babies with her handkerchief.)

Aunt Lill (to all who are studying this lesson):

Wu hocket dihr in eier Gmee? (*Where sit you in your church?* Where do you sit in your church?)

- An Amish girl has to remember to sit primly and keep her dress modestly in place. If she does not, her mom might reprimand her for being “gawwerich.”

Die Bank Wagge far die Gmee

Phonics Tip

The letters "ae" have either

- the short "a" sound like in "rap" (drawn out slightly).[49]
- almost a long "a" sound (drawn out slightly) like in "came."[50]

Listen to the CD for the correct pronunciation.

Daett (Dad) - say Datt   Maed (girls) - say made

Grammar Tip

In English, to talk about the future, we say we **want** to do something tomorrow or next week or next year, etc. In Pennsylvania German, talking about the future is done the same way. Use the verb "welle" (want) with the infinitive of the verb (the verb on top of the verb chart), plus an adverb or adverb phrase. If one wants to emphasize *when* or *where* something will be done, say the adverb *after* the first verb.

Verb	
welle (to want)	
ich	will
du	wit**t**
er, sie	will
mir	well**e**
dihr	well**et**
sie	well**e**

Verb	
schaffe (to work)	
ich	schaff
du	schaff**scht**
er, sie	schaff**t**
mir	schaff**e**
dihr	schaff**et**
sie	schaff**e**

→ mariye

Examples:

Ich **will schaffe** *mariye frieh. (*I want to work morning early*). **OR** Ich **will** mariye frieh **schaffe**. (*I want morning early to work*. I want to work tomorrow morning.)

Mir **welle** schpot **schaffe** mariye. (*We want late to work tomorrow.)* **OR** Mir **welle** mariye schpot **schaffe**. *(We want tomorrow late to work.* We want to work late tomorrow.)

*"Mariye frieh" means tomorrow morning.

Culture Tip

Church lasts about three hours. The preachers preach in mostly Pennsylvania German, but they quote from the High German Bible. Everyone sings from the *Ausbund*, an old German hymn book. The songs are sung very slowly. One song can last ten minutes!

After church, everybody eats a lunch of snitz pie, cheese, pickles, pickled red beets, homemade bread, peanut butter spread, cheese spread, butter, jam, and coffee. Then everyone visits awhile before it is time to go home.

Exercises

A. Use the verb chart to fill in the correct form of the verb "hocke."

1. Dihr ____________ mit die grossi Buwe.
2. Du ____________ mit der Omar.
3. Sie (they) ____________ mit ihre Maem.
4. Mir ____________ uff die Bank.
5. Sie (she) ____________ mit die Maed.
6. Er ____________ uff der Schockelschtuhl.
7. Ich ____________ mit die Katherine.

B. Translate the sentences in A.

Sie sin ready far die Gmee.

(die) Weschmachien [p] Weschmachiene washer 	(der) Munet month 
(die) Hosse pants 	(die) Woch [p] Woche week 
(der) Rock [p] Reck dress 	groh gray 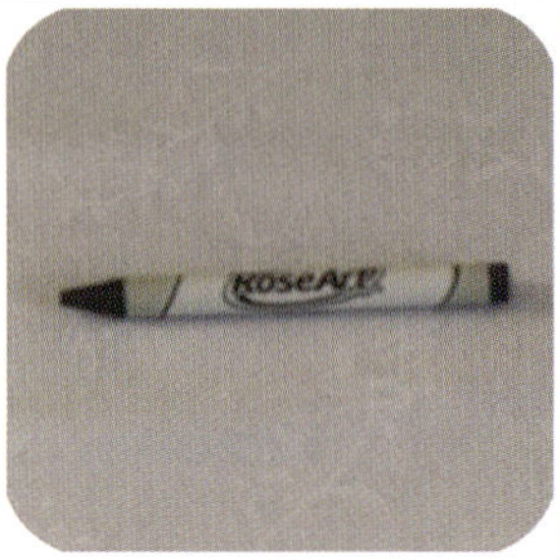
(es) Hemm [p] Hemmer shirt 	lodderich shaky loose rikety 

Other Words	
ab	off
wer	who

Verb	
wesche (to wash)	
ich	wesch
du	wesch**scht**
er, sie, es	wesch**t**
mir	wesch**e**
dihr	wesch**et**
sie	wesch**e**

Lesson 23 – Keeping Things Clean

John: Der Daett iss an schaffe heit. (Dad is working today.)

Susie: Die Schweschder Mary un der Bruder Jake sin an schpiele. (Sister Mary and Brother Jake are playing.) Ich bin an wesche. (I am washing.)

John: Du weschscht all die dreckichi Gleeder. (You wash all the dirty clothing.)

Susie: Ya, ich duh. (Yes, I do.) Die Hosse un die Hemmer sin als hesslich dreckich. (The pants and the shirts are usually terribly dirty.)

Die Reck sin net dreckich. (The dresses are not dirty.)

John: Die Weschmachien iss en glee Bissel lodderich. (The washer is a little bit rickety.) *Es iss alt. (It is old.)

Mom: Wer will es Dachweggeli ab wesche? (*Who wants the buggy off wash?* Who wants to wash off the buggy?)

John: Ich will! (I will.) Ich wesch es Dachweggeli! (*I wash the buggy.* I'll wash the buggy.)

Ich gleich es Dachweggeli ab wesche. (*I like the buggy off to wash.* I like to wash off the buggy.)

Susie: Mir wesche es alle Woch. (We wash it every week.)

Unser Dachweggeli iss groh. (Our buggy is gray.)

John: Die Dachweggelin in die Valley sin weiss. (The buggies in the valley are white.) Sell iss schpassich. (That is funny.)

Susie: Der John wescht aa der Schpring Waage. (*The John washes also the spring wagon.* John also washes the spring wagon.)

Er duht es recht. (He does it right.) Er iss pivvich. (He is particular.)

John: Es Uncle Omars un es Uncle Dans wesche net ihre Dachweggelin alle Woch. (*Uncle Omars and Uncle Dans wash not their buggies every week.* Uncle Omars and Uncle Dans do not wash their buggies every week.)

Susie: Sie wesche ihre Dachweggelin alle Munet. (They wash their buggies every month.) Sie sin net pivvich. (They are not particular.)

Aunt Lill (to all who are studying this lesson):

Weschet dihr eier Maschien alle Woch? (*Wash you your car every week?* Do you wash your car every week?)

*To make the pronoun agree with the noun, some speakers would say "Sie is alt" because "Weschmachien" is a feminine noun.

Phonics Tip

The letters "e" (when it is not short) and "ee," or "eh" have almost a long "a" sound (drawn out slightly) as in "came."[51] Listen to the CD for the correct pronunciation.

Examples:

glee (little) geh (go)

Grammar Tip

To say "I am working", "you are working", "they are working," etc. (present progressive), use the verb for "to be" from the first lesson, the word "an" and then the verb on top of the verb chart (the infinitive of the verb). Some Pennsylvania German speakers use the word "am" instead of "an."[52]

Verb	
sei (to be)	
ich	bin
du	bi**scht**
er, sie, es	iss
mir	sin
dihr	sin**t**
sie	sin

an

Verb	
schaffe (to work)	
ich	schaff
du	schaff**scht**
er, sie, es	schaff**t**
mir	schaff**e**
dihr	schaff**et**
sie	schaff**e**

Die Dachweggelin in die Valley sin weiss.

Examples:

Ich bin an schaffe. (I am working.)

Du bischt an esse. (You are eating.)

Er iss an lese. (He is reading.)

Mir sin an schpiele. (We are playing.)

Dihr sint an butze. (You are cleaning.)

Culture Tip

Many Amish people have wringer washers like this one. They are powered by gasoline engines or by air power.

There's a story about a kind Amish husband who decided to do the washing for his sick wife. Unfortunately, his long beard got caught in the wringer!

Exercises

A. Use the verb chart to fill in the correct form of the verb "wesche."

1. Dihr ____________ all die Eppel.
2. Er ____________ die Kieh.
3. Sie (they) ____________ die Benk eb die Gmee.
4. Mir ____________ all die Reck.
5. Sie (she) ____________ die Gleeder.
6. Ich ____________ es Bobbli ihre Schtuhl.
7. Du ____________ die Grummbiere eb Dinner.

B. Translate the sentences in A.

(die) Draub

[p] Drauwe

grape

(die) Fraa

woman[+]

wife

(der) Pasching

peach

(der) Schtor

[p] Schtore

store

(es) Mehl

flour

verdarewe

spoiled

(der) Zucker

sugar

Other Words	
wie viel	how many, how much
vielleicht	perhaps
noch	yet

Verb	
kaafe (to buy)	
ich	kaaf
du	kaaf**scht**
er, sie, es	kaaf**t**
mir	kaaf**e**
dihr	kaaf**et**
sie	kaaf**e**

Lesson 24 – Buying Groceries at the Store

Susie: Daer Appel iss schee. (This apple is nice.)
Selli Eppel sin aa schee. (Those apples are also nice.)

John: Ya, all vun die Eppel sin schee. (Yes, all of the apples are nice.)
Ich kaaf fimf vun die. (I buy five of these.)

Susie: Die Pasching sin aa schee. (These peaches are also nice.)
Wie viel welle mir? (*How many want we?* How many do we want?)

John: Vielleicht zehe. (Maybe ten.) Mir kaafe zehe Pasching. (We buy ten peaches.)

Susie: Do sin deel Drauwe. (Here are some grapes.) Sie sin schee. (They are nice.)
Kaafscht du deel vun die? (*Buy you some of these?* Do you buy some of these?)

John: Ya, ich duh. (Yes, I do.) Ich kaaf drei bunches vun die. (I buy three bunches of these.)

Susie: Datt iss en Fraa mit drei Kinner. (There is a woman with three children.)
Sie kaaft en lot Groceries. (*She buys a lot groceries.* She buys a lot of groceries.) Ihre Kinner sin verdarewe. (Her children are spoiled.)

John: Ya, sie weller yuscht Candy un Soda. (*Yes, they want just candy and soda.* Yes, they just want candy and soda.)
Sie welle net Fruit un Vegetables. (*They want not fruit and vegetables.* They do not want fruit and vegetables.)

Susie: Datt iss en Grossdaadi un en Grossmammi. (There is a Grandfather and a Grandmother.) Sie kaafe en lot Fruit. (*They buy a lot fruit.* They buy a lot of fruit.)

John: Mir welle noch Mehl un Zucker kaafe. (*We want yet flour and sugar to buy*. We want to buy flour and sugar yet.)

Susie: Ya, die Maem will Mehl un Zucker far Cookies mache. (*Yes, Mom wants flour and sugar for cookies to make.* Yes, Mom wants flour and sugar to make cookies.)

Aunt Lill (to all who are studying this lesson):
Was kaafet dihr an der Schtor? (*What buy you at the store?* What do you buy at the store?)

Sie gehn zu der Schtor mit en Dachweggeli.

Phonics Tip

The letters "o" (when it is not short) and "oo" or "oh" have almost the "oo" sound as in "cook" (drawn out slightly). Listen to the CD for the correct pronunciation.

Examples:

rot (red) Brot (bread)

The "o" in these examples follow the short vowel sound rules, but they are still long.

Grammar Tips

In the last lessons, to say "this" and "that," we used the words "des" and "sell." They were being used as pronouns.

Examples:

Ich will *des*. (I want this.) Du gleichscht *sell*. (You like that.)

Using "sell" as an adjective follows the rules we learned in Lesson 9. It gets more complicated when using **"des"** as an *adjective*. In this lesson we have the sentence, "Daer Abbel iss schee." We use "daer" instead of "des" because "Abbel" is masculine.

Use the chart below to help you.[53] Don't worry about perfection. If someone says "seller" instead of "selli," people will still understand. Communication is getting the point across!

	masculine	feminine	neuter		plural
that	**seller**	**selli**	**sell**	those	**selli**
this	**daer**	**die**	**des**	these	**die**

Examples:

Ich will **seller** Pasching. (I want that peach.) "Pasching" is masculine so we use "seller," which is also masculine.

Die Millich iss gut. (This milk is good.) "Millich" is feminine so we use "die," which is also feminine.

Culture Tip

Amish shop at normal stores just like everyone else. Most stores in Lancaster County have hitching rails or even a small shed especially for the Amish shoppers. When Amish children go shopping with their parents, they are usually exceptionally well behaved, although they might stare at the "English" shoppers!

Exercises

A. Use the verb chart to fill in the correct form of the verb "kaafe."

1. Du ____________ Eppel far Eppel Boi mache.
2. Sie (she) ____________ en Hinkel far Dinner.
3. Ich ____________ en Licht far die Kich.
4. Sie (they) ____________ Babier far Briefe schreiwe.
5. Er ____________ Bicher.
6. Dihr ____________ Ess-sach.
7. Mir ____________ en Bett.

B. Translate the sentences in A.

Sie gehn zu der Schtor mit en Driver.

(der) Winder [p] Windere winter		(es) Feld [p] Felder field	
(es) Friehyaahr [p] Friehyaahre spring		(der) Esel mule[+]	
(der) Summer [p] Summere summer		(die) Tomaets tomato	
(der) Herbscht [p] Herbschte fall		(die) Supp soup	

Other Words	
verbei	past
erscht	first

Verb	
zehle (to intend)	
ich	zehl
du	zehl**scht**
er, sie, es	zehl**t**
mir	zehl**e**
dihr	zehl**et**
sie	zehl**e**

Lesson 25 – Seasons

John: Der Winder iss verbei. (The winter is past.)

Susie: Nau iss es Frieyaahr. (Now it is spring.)

Was zehlscht du duh heit? (What will you do today?)

John: Ich zehl schaffe in die Felder. (I will work in the fields.)

Ich zehl schaffe mit zwee Geil. (I will work with two horses.)

Ich zehl net schaffe mit die Esel. (I will not work with the mules.)

Mir zehle en lot Arwet duh. (*We will a lot work do.* We will do a lot of work.)

Susie: Glei iss es Summer. (*Soon is it summer.* Soon it is summer.)

John: Schpeeder iss es Herbscht. (*Later is it fall.* Later it is fall.)

Susie, was zehlscht du duh heit? (Susie, what will you do today?)

Susie: Ich zehl es erscht Dinner mache. (*I will the first dinner make.* I will first make dinner.)

Ich zehl tomaets Supp mache. (*I will tomato soup make.* I will make tomato soup.)

Mariye zehle der Grossdaadi un ich fatt geh. (*Tomorrow will the Grandfather and I away go*. Tomorrow Grandfather and I will go away.)

John: Ya, dihr zehlet zu die Geil Vendyu geh. (*Yes, you will to the horse auction go*. Yes, you will go to the horse auction.)

Susie: Die Vendyu iss Schpass! (The auction is fun.)

Aunt Lill (to all who are studying this this lesson):

Zehlet dihr meh Pennsylvania Deitsch schtudie?

(*Will you more Pennsylvania German study?* Will you study more Pennsylvania German?)

Er schafft mit zwee Geil.

Sie iss mit der Grossdaadi an die Vendyu.

Phonics Tip

The letters "u" (when it is not short) and "uu," or "uh" have the "oo" sound as in "boot."[54]

Examples:

kuh (cow) buwe (boy)

Grammar Tip

In Lesson 22, we learned that sometimes the verb "welle" is used to talk about the future. Another verb to talk about the future is "zehle," which means "intend to" or "will." It is usually followed by another verb on the top of the chart (the infinitive). The adverb or adverb phrase can go between the two verbs or after the second verb.

Verb	
zehle (to intend)	
ich	zehl
du	zehl**scht**
er, sie	zehl**t**
mir	zehl**e**
dihr	zehl**et**
sie	zehl**e**

Verb	
schaffe (to work)	
ich	schaff
du	schaff**scht**
er, sie, es	schaff**t**
mir	schaff**e**
dihr	schaff**et**
sie	schaff**e**

Examples:

Ich **zehl schaffe** mariye. (I intend to work tomorrow.) OR Ich **zehl** mariye **schaffe**. (*I intend to tomorrow work.* I intend to work tomorrow.)

Du **zehlscht** in es Feld **schaffe**. (*You will in the field work.* You will work in the field.) OR Du **zehlscht schaffe** in es Feld. (You will work in the field.)

Er **zehlt schaffe**. (He intends to work.)

Culture Tip

For Amish children, going to the animal auction is like going to a fair. They can watch the animals being sold, and Dad might give them money for a hot dog and soda. If they are very lucky, they might come home with a pony!

For the old men, the auction is a place to socialize. They catch up with the latest news or play checkers.

Exercises

A. Use the verb chart to fill in the correct form of the verb "zehle."

1. Sie (she) ____________ fatt geh mit der Gaul.
2. Er ____________ schaffe in es Feld.
3. Du ____________ frieh esse.
4. Sie (they) ____________ schpiele mit die Dallbobbe.
5. Dihr ____________ eier Arwet duh.
6. Ich ____________ en Buch lese.
7. Mir ____________ schtudie mariye.

B. Translate the sentences in A.

Die Geil Vendyu

Here is one last essential verb to know to say something very important!

Verb	
schwetze (to speak)	
ich	schwetz
du	schwetz**scht**
er, sie, es	schwetz**t**
mir	schwetz**e**
dihr	schwetz**et**
sie	schwetz**e**

Ich schwetz Pennsylvania Deitch!

(I speak Pennsylvania German.)

Ich schwetz en Bissel Pennsylvania Deitch.

(I speak a little Pennsylvania German.)

Congratulations!

Learning More Pennsylvania German Verbs

In the back of the book are two empty verb charts. Copy them and ask a native speaker about a verb you want to learn. For example, you decide to learn the verb "think." Ask the native speaker, "How do you say 'I think' in Pennsylvania German?" Then ask, "How do you say, 'You think' in Pennsylvania German?" and so on until the chart is complete.

Hint: For regular verbs, the verb on top of the chart is the same verb you use for "mir" and "sie."

Growing Your Pennsylvania German Vocabulary

If your grandmother or cousin or neighbor is a native speaker, learn new words from them. Buy a little notebook like the one in the picture. Make tabs with heavy paper for different sections. The sections could be labeled FOOD, PEOPLE, OTHER NOUNS, ADJECTIVES, ADVERBS, or whatever labels make sense to you. Draw a line down the page, about one-third from the left side, so you have room to add "die," "der," or "es," and the plural of the word on the right side if necessary.

Ask a native speaker how to say a word (or buy a good Pennsylvania German dictionary), and then write it in your book. The native speaker will probably not know how to spell the word because most Pennsylvania German speakers never formally study the language! Do not worry too much about the spelling; just write the word in a way that you can remember.

One caution about the dictionary: Amish speakers use a lot of English loan words so some of the words in the dictionary may not be words they actually use in everyday speech.

To study your little notebook, cover the Pennsylvania German side and see if you can remember the words. If you do this over and over, you will soon recall the words quickly.

Submit your language tips to www.speakingamish.com and we may add them to the website. Keep checking the website for other new and fun things.

Endnotes

[1] J. William Frey. *A Simple Grammar of Pennsylvania Dutch* (Ashfield: Stine, 2008), p. 4.

[2] Ibid, p. 5.

[3] Ibid, p. 10.

[4] Ibid, pp. 4-5.

[5] Ibid, p. 4.

[6] Ibid, p. 5.

[7] Ibid, p. 45.

[8] Joshua R. Brown and Douglas J. Madenford. *Schwetz Mol Deitsch.* (Millersville: Center for Pennsylvania German Studies, 2009), p. 11.

[9] Ibid.

[10] J. William Frey. *A Simple Grammar of Pennsylvania Dutch* (Ashfield: Stine, 2008), p. 45.

[11] Ibid, p. 3.

[12] Ibid. pp. 53-54.

[13] Ibid, p. 3.

[14] Ibid, pp. 2-3.

[15] Ibid, p. 18.

[16] Ibid.

[17] Ibid.

[18] Joshua R. Brown and Douglas J. Madenford. *Schwetz Mol Deitsch.* (Millersville: Center for Pennsylvania German Studies, 2009), p. 147.

[19] Ibid.

[20] J. William Frey. *A Simple Grammar of Pennsylvania Dutch* (Ashfield: Stine, 2008), p. 19.

[21] Ibid, p. 3.

[22] Ibid.

[23] Joshua R. Brown and Douglas J. Madenford. *Schwetz Mol Deitsch.* (Millersville: Center for Pennsylvania German Studies, 2009), p. 147.

[24] J. William Frey. *A Simple Grammar of Pennsylvania Dutch* (Ashfield: Stine, 2008), p. 5.

[25] Ibid.

[26] Ibid.

[27] "German for Beginners: Pronunciation - *Aussprache* (Part 3)." About.com.

[28] Joshua R. Brown and Douglas J. Madenford. *Schwetz Mol Deitsch*. (Millersville: Center for Pennsylvania German Studies, 2009), p. 30.

[29] J. William Frey. *A Simple Grammar of Pennsylvania Dutch* (Ashfield: Stine, 2008), p. 2.

[30] Joshua R. Brown and Douglas J. Madenford. *Schwetz Mol Deitsch*. (Millersville: Center for Pennsylvania German Studies, 2009), p. 30.

[31] J. William Frey. *A Simple Grammar of Pennsylvania Dutch* (Ashfield: Stine, 2008), p. 4.

[32] Ibid, p. 1.

[33] Ibid.

[34] Ibid.

[35] Ibid.

[36] Ibid.

[37] Ibid.

[38] Ibid, p. 44.

[39] Ibid, p. 44-45.

[40] Ibid, p. 1.

[41] Ibid.

[42] Ibid.

[43] Ibid.

[44] Ibid

[45] Ibid.

[46] Ibid.

[47] Ibid.

[48] Ibid.

[49] Ibid.

[50] Ibid, p. 2.

[51] Ibid.

[52] Joshua R. Brown and Douglas J. Madenford. *Schwetz Mol Deitsch*. (Millersville: Center for Pennsylvania German Studies, 2009), p. 73.

[53] J. William Frey. *A Simple Grammar of Pennsylvania Dutch* (Ashfield: Stine, 2008), p. 23.

[54] Ibid, p. 2.

Bibliography

Beam, C. Richard, and Jennifer L. Trout. *The Comprehensive Pennsylvania German Dictionary*. 11 vols. Millersville: Center for Pennsylvania German Studies, 2006. Print.

Brown, Joshua R., and Douglas J. Madenford. *Schwetz Mol Deitsch*. Millersville: Center for Pennsylvania German Studies, 2009. Print.

Frey, J. William. *A Simple Grammar of Pennsylvania Dutch*. Lancaster: Brookshire Printing, 1985. Print.

"German for Beginners: Pronunciation - *Aussprache* (Part 3)." *About.com German Language.* About.com. Web. 4 Feb. 2013.

Stine, Eugene E. *Pennsylvania German Dictionary*. Ashfield: Stine, 2008. Print.

Phonics Chart

	English Equivalent	Lesson
r in the beginning of a word or between two vowels	r	1
r (non-Lancaster areas)	Spanish rolled r	1
w	v	1
r in the middle or end of a word	ah	2
r following the short "a" sound and preceding a consonant	silent	4
sch	sh	5
ch after ei, ie, or i	h	6
ch after a, o, or ou	guttural h	6
b, **d**, and **g** in the end of a word	p, t, k	7
g or **gg** in the middle of a word	almost a w or y	8
bb and **dd** in the middle of a word	p, t	10
v	f	11
z and **tz**	ts	12
h following a vowel	silent	13
aa	aw	14
au	almost like the "o" sound in "tot," but more drawn out	15
chs	x	16
short vowels		
a	o sound in "hop"	17
e	e sound in "ten"	18
i	i sound in "big"	19
o	u sound in "cut"	20
u	oo sound in "book"	21
long vowels		
ei and ie	long i and long e	9
ae	either the short a sound in "rap" (drawn out slightly) or the long a sound (drawn out slightly) in "came"	22
e, ee, and eh	almost the long a sound (drawn out slightly) in "came"	23
o, oo, and oh	almost the oo sound in "cook"	24
u, uu, and uh	the oo sound in "boot"	25

Verb Charts

Lesson 1, 2, 3, 4

May be copied for personal use.

sei (to be)	
ich	bin
du	bi**scht**
er, sie, es	iss
mir	sin
dihr	sin**t**
sie	si**n**

gleich (to like)	
ich	gleich
du	gleich**scht**
er, sie, es	gleich**t**
mir	gleich**e**
dihr	gleich**et**
sie	gleich**e**

hawwe (to have)	
ich	hab (hawwich)
du	ho**scht**
er, sie, es	ho**t**
mir	he**n**
dihr	he**nt**
sie	he**n**

geh (to go)	
ich	geh (gehn ich)
du	geh**scht**
er, sie, es	geh**t**
mir	geh**n**
dihr	geh**nt**
sie	geh**n**

Verb Charts

Lesson 5, 6, 7, 8

May be copied for personal use.

schaffe (to work)	
ich	schaff
du	schaff**scht**
er, sie, es	schaff**t**
mir	schaff**e**
dihr	schaff**et**
sie	schaff**e**

esse (to eat)	
ich	ess
du	ess**scht**
er, sie, es	ess**t**
mir	ess**e**
dihr	ess**et**
sie	ess**e**

schtudie (to study)	
ich	schtudi
du	schtudi**scht**
er, sie, es	schtudi**t**
mir	schtudi**e**
dihr	schtudi**et**
sie	schtudi**e**

duh (to do)	
ich	duh (duhn ich)
du	du**scht**
er, sie, es	dut**t**
mir	die**n**
dihr	die**nt**
sie	die**n**

Verb Charts

Lesson 9, 10, 11, 12

May be copied for personal use.

lese (to read)	
ich	lees
du	lee**scht**
er, sie, es	lees**t**
mir	les**e**
dihr	les**et**
sie	les**e**

schpiele (to play)	
ich	schpiel
du	schpiel**scht**
er, sie, es	schpiel**t**
mir	schpiel**e**
dihr	schpiel**et**
sie	schpiel**e**

schreiwe (to write)	
ich	schreib
du	schreib**scht**
er, sie, es	schreib**t**
mir	schreiw**e**
dihr	schreiw**et**
sie	schreiw**e**

sehne (to see)	
ich	sehn
du	sehn**scht**
er, sie, es	sehn**t**
mir	sehn**e**
dihr	sehn**et**
sie	sehn**e**

Verb Charts

Lesson 13, 14, 15, 16

May be copied for personal use.

schlofe (to sleep)	
ich	schlof
du	schlof**scht**
er, sie, es	schlof**t**
mir	schlof**e**
dihr	schlof**et**
sie	schlof**e**

schteh (to stand)	
ich	schteh (schtehn ich)
du	schteh**scht**
er, sie, es	schteh**t**
mir	schtehn
dihr	schtehn**t**
sie	schtehn

butze (to clean)	
ich	butz
du	butz**scht**
er, sie, es	butz**t**
mir	butz**e**
dihr	butz**et**
sie	butz**e**

welle (to want)	
ich	will
du	wit**t**
er, sie, es	will
mir	well**e**
dihr	well**et**
sie	well**e**

Verb Charts

Lesson 17, 18, 19, 20

May be copied for personal use.

wuhne (to live)	
ich	wuhn
du	wuhn**scht**
er, sie, es	wuhn**t**
mir	wuhn**e**
dihr	wuhn**et**
sie	wuhn**e**

kumme (to come)	
ich	kumm
du	kumm**scht**
er, sie, es	kumm**t**
mir	kumm**e**
dihr	kumm**et**
sie	kumm**e**

mache (to make)	
ich	mach
du	mach**scht**
er, sie, es	mach**t**
mir	mach**e**
dihr	mach**et**
sie	mach**e**

gewwe (to give)	
ich	geb
du	geb**scht**
er, sie, es	geb**t**
mir	geww**e**
dihr	geww**et**
sie	geww**e**

Verb Charts

Lesson 21, 22, 23, 24

May be copied for personal use.

laafe (to walk)	
ich	laaf
du	laaf**scht**
er, sie, es	laaf**t**
mir	laaf**e**
dihr	laaf**et**
sie	laaf**e**

hocke (to sit)	
ich	hock
du	hock**scht**
er, sie, es	hock**t**
mir	hock**e**
dihr	hock**et**
sie	hock**e**

wesch (to wash)	
ich	wesch
du	wesch**scht**
er, sie, es	wesch**t**
mir	wesch**e**
dihr	wesch**et**
sie	wesch**e**

kaafe (to buy)	
ich	kaaf
du	kaaf**scht**
er, sie, es	kaaf**t**
mir	kaaf**e**
dihr	kaaf**et**
sie	kaaf**e**

Verb Charts

Lesson 25, extra

May be copied for personal use.

zehle (to intend)	
ich	zehl
du	zehl**scht**
er, sie, es	zehl**t**
mir	zehl**e**
dihr	zehl**et**
sie	zehl**e**

schwetz (to speak)	
ich	schwetz
du	schwetz**scht**
er, sie, es	schwetz**t**
mir	schwetz**e**
dihr	schwetz**et**
sie	schwetz**e**

ich	
du	
er, sie, es	
mir	
dihr	
sie	

ich	
du	
er, sie, es	
mir	
dihr	
sie	

Answers for Exercises

Lesson 1

A.

1. der
2. die
3. die
4. der

B.

(Individual answers)

C.

1. bin
2. sin
3. iss
4. sint
5. iss
6. bischt
7. sin

Lesson 2

A.

1. gleich
2. gleiche
3. gleicht
4. gleichet
5. gleicht
6. gleichscht
7. gleiche

B.

1. I like cake.
2. We like apples.
3. She likes Dad.
4. You like cookies.
5. He likes pie.
6. You like pudding.
7. They like food.

Lesson 3

A.

1. hab
2. hen
3. hot
4. hent
5. hen
6. hoscht
7. hot

B.

1. Ich hab net drei Kuche.
2. Sie hen net en Maschien.
3. Dihr hent net acht Nochbere.

C.

1. I don't have three cakes.
2. They don't have a car.
3. You don't have eight neighbors.

Lesson 4

A.

1. geh
2. gehnt
3. geht
4. gehn
5. gehn
6. gehscht
7. geht

B.

1. Sie gleiche en Schpring Waage net.
2. Er gleicht Eppel net.
3. Ich gleich Shoo-fly Boi net.

C.

1. They don't like a spring wagon.
2. He doesn't like apples.
3. I don't like shoo-fly pie.

Lesson 5

A.

1. schaff
2. schaffe
3. schaffe
4. schafft
5. schaffet
6. schaffscht
7. schafft

B.

1. Ebmols bin ich langsam. (Sometimes I am slow.)
2. Allfatt schaffe sie hatt. (They always work hard.)

Lesson 6

A.

1. ess
2. esse
3. esst
4. esset
5. esse
6. esscht
7. esst

B.

1. Esscht du gschtampti Grummbiere? (Do you eat mashed potatoes?)
2. Esst er en lot Kuche? (Does he eat a lot of cake?)

Lesson 7

A.

1. schtudit
2. schtudit
3. schtudi
4. schtudischt
5. schtudie
6. schtudiet
7. schtudie

B.

1. She studies in school.
2. He studies the book.
3. I study with the children.
4. You do not study in German.
5. We study together.
6. You study hard sometimes.
7. They study the books.

Lesson 8

A.

1. dutt
2. dient
3. dien
4. duscht
5. dien
6. dutt
7. duh

B.

1. She does nice work.
2. You do good work.
3. They do the books.
4. You do everything right.
5. We do sloppy work.
6. He doesn't do good work.
7. I do it right.

Lesson 9

A.

1. er
2. (no ending)
3. i
4. er
5. ner
6. (no ending)
7. (no ending)

B.

1. He is a smart farmer.
2. We have a big book.
3. They have a loud car.
4. You have a loud horse.
5. It is a small apple.
6. You like a big light.
7. I like a nice buggy.

Lesson 10

A.

1. schpielscht
2. schpiele
3. schpielet
4. schpielt
5. schpielt
6. schpiel
7. schpiele

B.

1. Ebmols schpiele sie mit unser Dollboppe.
2. Allfatt schpiel ich mit die Susie.
3. Ebmols schpielt er mit die Kinner.

Lesson 11

A.

1. schreib
2. schreibscht
3. schreiwe
4. schreibt
5. schreiwe
6. schreibt
7. schreiwet

B.

(suggested verbs)

1. schreiwe
2. schaffe
3. schpiele
4. schaffe
5. esse

Lesson 12

A.

1. sehnt
2. sehnscht
3. sehnt
4. sehn
5. sehne
6. sehne
7. sehnet

B.

1. He sees the car.
2. You see all the apples.
3. She sees the little children.
4. I see the slŏppy work.
5. We see the cows.
6. They see our chickens.
7. You see their/her buggy.

Lesson 13

A.

1. schlof
2. schlofscht
3. schloft
4. schlofe
5. schlofe
6. schloft
7. schlofe

B.

1. I sleep in the bed.
2. You don't sleep at school.
3. She sleeps with the baby.
4. They sleep well.
5. We don't sleep in the morning.
6. He sleeps in the room.
7. You don't sleep in the barn.

Lesson 14

A.

1. schtehn
2. schtehscht
3. schtehn
4. schteht
5. schtehn
6. schteh
7. schteht

B.

1. You get up before the sun.
2. You get up after me.
3. They get up late.
4. He stands on an apple. He is funny.
5. We get up early.
6. I stand on the dirt.
7. She gets up early in the morning.

Lesson 15

A.

1. butzet
2. butzscht
3. butzt
4. butze
5. butze
6. butzt
7. butz

B.

1. You clean the house.
2. You clean the buggy.
3. He cleans his car.
4. They clean the school.
5. We clean our barn.
6. She cleans her room.
7. I clean all the corners.

Lesson 16

A.

1. welle
2. will
3. will
4. wellet
5. welle
6. witt
7. will

B.

1. They want five beds.
2. She wants apple sauce.
3. He wants a cow.
4. You want a big horse.
5. We want a clock.
6. You want nine potatoes.
7. I want a little chicken.

Lesson 17

A.

1. wuhnet
2. wuhnscht
3. wuhnt
4. wuhne
5. wuhne
6. wuhnt
7. wuhn

B.

1. Die Mary ihre Haus iss schee.
2. Der John sei Gaul iss gross.
3. Die Nochbere ihre Scheier iss sauwer.

Lesson 18

A.

1. kummet
2. kummt
3. kumme
4. kumm
5. kumme
6. kummt
7. kummscht

B.

1. You come before breakfast.
2. He comes for supper.
3. They come to our house.
4. I come with a buggy.
5. We come with a horse.
6. She comes tomorrow.
7. You come to church.

Lesson 19

A.

1. machet
2. mache
3. macht
4. mache
5. machscht
6. macht
7. mach

B.

1. You make nice quilts.
2. We make mashed potatoes for dinner.
3. He makes buggies.
4. They make cheese with milk.
5. You make apple pie for supper.
6. She makes apple sauce with her children.
7. I make a loaf of bread.

Lesson 20

A.

1. gebt
2. geb
3. gebt
4. gewwet
5. gewwe
6. gewwe
7. gebscht

B.

1. She gives the baby milk.
2. I give him a loaf of bread.
3. He gives cows to the poor people.
4. You give the children cookies.
5. They give us change.
6. We give them/her shoo-fly pie.
7. You give money to the man.

Lesson 21

A.

1. laaft
2. laafscht
3. laaft
4. laafet
5. laaf
6. laafe
7. laafe

B.

1. He walks fast.
2. You walk slowly.
3. She walks with him.
4. You walk because their place is near.
5. I walk to the neighbors.
6. We walk to school.
7. They walk with us.

Lesson 22

A.

1. hocket
2. hockscht
3. hocke
4. hocke
5. hockt
6. hockt
7. hock

B.

1. You sit with the big boys.
2. You sit with Omar.
3. They sit with their Mom.
4. We sit on the bench.
5. She sits with the girls.
6. He sits on the rocking chair.
7. I sit with Katherine.

Lesson 23

A.

1. weschet
2. wescht
3. weschet
4. wesche
5. wescht
6. wesch
7. weschscht

B.

1. You wash all the apples.
2. He washes the cows.
3. They wash all the benches before church.
4. We wash all the dresses.
5. She washes the clothes.
6. I wash the baby's chair.
7. You wash the potatoes before dinner.

Lesson 24

A.

1. kaafscht
2. kaaft
3. kaaf
4. kaafe
5. kaaft
6. kaafet
7. kaafe

B.

1. You buy apples to make apple pie.
2. She buys a chicken for dinner.
3. I buy a light for the kitchen.
4. They buy paper to write letters.
5. He buys books.
6. You buy food.
7. We buy a bed.

Lesson 25

A.

1. zehlt
2. zehlt
3. zehlscht
4. zehle
5. zehlet
6. zehl
7. zehle

B.

1. She will go away with the horse.
2. He will work in the field.
3. You will eat early.
4. They will play with the dolls.
5. You will do your work.
6. I will read a book.
7. We will study tomorrow.